Terra Non Firma

Several old buildings in Coalinga, California, collapsed or suffered major damage during the earthquake of May 2, 1983 (magnitude 6.5). This scene will be repeated in many other cities in the years ahead.

Terra Non Firma

Understanding and Preparing for Earthquakes

James M. Gere
Haresh C. Shah

W.H. Freeman and Company
New York

This book was published originally as a part of *The Portable Stanford*, a series of books published by the Stanford Alumni Association, Stanford, California.

Library of Congress Cataloging in Publication Data

Gere, James M.
  Terra Non Firma.

  Reprint. Originally published: Stanford, Calif.:
Stanford Alumni Association, 1984. (The Portable
Stanford)
  Includes index.
  1. Earthquakes. I. Shah, Haresh C. II. Title.
QE534.2.G47 1984   363.3'495   84-6007
ISBN 0-7167-1496-5
ISBN 0-7167-1497-3 (pbk.)

Printed in the United States of America

9 8 7 6 5 4 3 2 1   ML   1 0 8 9 8 7 6 5 4 3

Contents

Preface

THE EARTHQUAKE HAZARD in the United States becomes more severe as each day passes without a major earthquake. The press, radio, and television do an excellent job of alerting the public to the hazard through news reports, feature articles, and television specials. Nature also provides us with regular reminders of the dangers, catching us unprepared when it strikes communities such as Challis, Idaho (October 1983), and Coalinga, California (May 1983).

This increased awareness of the threat has prompted many people to seek additional information about earthquakes and to ask questions about what they should do. Almost every day we receive phone calls from homeowners, business executives, and school officials who are anxious to know what they can do to reduce deaths, injuries, and property damage in the next earthquake. Our aim in this book is to answer the questions that most people have.

To provide an understanding of earthquakes, we begin by explaining their causes and their effects (Chapters 1 through 6). Then we discuss preparing for earthquakes at the engineering, community, and personal levels (Chapters 7 through 9). With this background, you should be able to make intelligent decisions related to your own safety, the safety of those around you, and the reduction of property losses.

As engineering professors at Stanford, we usually write technical material for students, researchers, and practicing engineers. However, in this book we have tried to tell you what you need to know about earthquakes *without* being technical. The book is based upon many years of practical experience in coping with the problems caused by earthquakes, both in the United States and abroad. We have learned about some earthquakes through reports and interviews; we have studied others by actually visiting the sites—such as Coalinga, California (1983), El Asnam, Algeria (1980), Tangshan, China (1976), Guatemala (1976), Managua, Nicaragua (1972), and San Fernando, California (1971).

We wish to express our sincere thanks to those in the Portable Stanford series who helped in the preparation of this book, especially editor Miriam Miller and production manager Laura Ackerman-Shaw, who patiently improved our presentation and carried this book to completion. We are also indebted to former editor Cynthia Fry Gunn for getting the book started, to Tom Lewis for creating the cover and the centerfold map, and to Donna Salmon for drawing the figures. Our thanks also to Isabelle Fox for several discussions of the psychological effects of the San Fernando earthquake; to Elisa Bosley, Camilla Graham, and Thea Kennedy for office assistance and typing; and to our wives, Janice Gere and Joan Shah, for critical discussions of the manuscript.

Numerous earthquake engineers and seismologists have indirectly contributed their knowledge and experience to this book. They include practicing engineers, university colleagues, and researchers—in this country and around the world. We are especially grateful to the National Science Foundation, which, through its Earthquake Hazards Mitigation Program, has been the principal supporter of our research, and to Donald G. MacKay, Kenneth Medearis, and others who have provided us with generous financial support for our educational program.

One person who stands out as the source of great inspiration to us over the years is Dr. John A. Blume, structural engineer, a friend and counselor as well as benefactor. We take great pride in our association with the laboratory on the Stanford University campus that bears his name—The John A. Blume Earthquake Engineering Center—and we respectfully dedicate this book to him.

James M. Gere
Haresh C. Shah

Stanford University
April 1984

Terra Non Firma

The great Lisbon earthquake of 1755 surprised a population gathered in the city's churches on All Saints' Day. (Courtesy of USGS)

1

A Shaky Experience

They felt the earth quake underfoot; the sea was lashed into a froth, burst into the port, and smashed all the vessels lying at anchor there. Whirlwinds of fire and ash swirled through the streets and public squares; houses crumbled, roofs came crashing down on foundations, foundations split; thirty thousand inhabitants . . . were crushed in the ruins.

"The Last Judgment is here," cried Candide.

—Voltaire, *Candide* (on the
1755 Lisbon earthquake)

THERE MAY COME A TIME when any one of us will experience a terrifying and humbling reminder of Nature's power. Earthquakes, tornadoes, hurricanes, and floods remain "acts of God," and we are as helpless to prevent them today as were our distant ancestors in the pre-scientific past. We may not decide, with Candide, that "the Last Judgment is here," though we may for a moment feel that our end is at hand.

The likelihood that you will feel an earthquake is actually very high. It happens to most people several times during their lives, and for many, the experience is indeed serious. On a worldwide basis, about one person in 8,000 will end his life in an earthquake, and ten times that many will be injured by an earthquake sometime during their lives.

The major seismic zones of the world are shown on the centerfold map. If you live in one of these zones, you probably have already experienced an earthquake. Within the United States, most Californians can claim that distinction. A typical resident of Los Angeles will be shaken several times in a lifetime, at least once by a very damaging earthquake. In contrast, there are portions of a few states (such as Texas and Florida) where earthquakes are virtually unknown.

About 70 million people in the United States live in regions where the earthquake hazard can be classified as "severe," that is, where damaging earthquakes occur at least once in a lifetime. Another 120 million live in regions where the hazard is "moderate," and the remainder can safely ignore the earthquake hazard (until they decide to travel).

If It Happens to You

If you haven't yet had this shaky experience, try to imagine what it is like to be caught in an earthquake. Perhaps you are sitting at a desk or table when the earthquake comes. It catches you completely by surprise, and the first jolt makes you sit upright and say, "What was that?" Many thoughts go through your mind as you try to grasp the situation. "Did a big truck go by? Did something drop?" As the shaking motion continues, you quickly realize that it is not a bump but an actual earthquake, and you immediately have frightening thoughts: "Is the shaking going to last long? Why doesn't it stop? Is the building going to fall down? What should I do?"

It takes only a few seconds for these questions to go through your mind. If the shaking stops promptly, you feel great relief. But if it continues, your heart begins to pound and you instinctively do *something*, even if it is the wrong thing. Some people shriek and shout, some run for the exits, and some freeze with fright. After all, the floors on which we tread are supposed to be secure, like terra firma, and it is truly frightening when that feeling of security is taken from us. If you have planned ahead for this emergency, you move to a safe spot, preferably under a table or desk, and calmly tell others to do the same.

After a few seconds of shaking, the damage begins. Window glass cracks and breaks, objects fall off the shelves, bookcases topple, light fixtures fall from the ceilings, and cracks appear in walls, floors, and ceilings. The noise is deafening. It takes only a dozen seconds of strong shaking to wreck an entire building, sometimes even bringing it to the ground. The longer the shaking continues, the more severe the damage.

When it is finally over, you are amazed to learn how brief the earthquake really was. When questioned afterward about how long the shaking lasted, people estimate 30 to 40 seconds for an earthquake that in reality lasted 5 to 10 seconds. We also exaggerate the amount of movement because the human body is extremely sensitive to motion of the ground. Consider, for example, how readily we feel the motion of the ground caused by a truck passing nearby, although the actual ground displacement may be less than a millimeter.* When asked how much their building moved during an

_____
* One millimeter equals approximately 1/25 of an inch; to obtain inches, multiply the number of millimeters by 1/25 (or 0.04).

The roof and floors of this building pancaked during the 1972 Managua, Nicaragua, earthquake.

earthquake, people will say, "It swayed back and forth two or three feet," when it actually swayed less than an inch. An extreme example of how misleading one's senses can be was related to us by an engineer in Turkey. In the course of investigating an earthquake that shook Istanbul, he talked with a muezzin who had been calling the faithful to prayers from the top of a minaret when the earthquake struck. The muezzin insisted that the minaret swayed so much that he could touch the ground as it went back and forth.

Building Safety

What happens to you during an earthquake depends upon how far you are from the source of the earthquake, how long the shaking lasts, the construction of the building you are in, the soil and foundation conditions under the building, and many other factors. In countries such as the United States, where most people live in wood-frame houses or well-constructed apartment buildings, you are safest if an earthquake occurs at night when you are at home. Little harm can come to you because such houses and buildings hold together remarkably well. Also, at home there usually is no heavy machinery, equipment, or furniture to fall on you—unless you unwisely have placed a heavy hi-fi set on a shelf above your bed.

In those countries where unreinforced adobe and masonry construction is prevalent, the situation is reversed and nighttime earthquakes usually cause the greatest loss of life—the thick walls and heavy roofs of mud or tile collapse directly onto the occupants. In Guatemala in 1976 an earthquake of magnitude 7.5 took place at three o'clock in the morning, killing about 23,000 people and leaving a million homeless. Most of the deaths occurred in rural villages, where the houses collapsed in ruins. In Nicaragua in 1972 another nighttime earthquake caused more than 5,000 deaths; this earthquake had a magnitude of 6.2. Similar disasters occur every few years around the world, the greatest being the Tangshan, China, earthquake of 1976, which struck at 3:42 A.M. and killed more than a quarter of a million people (see page 134). By contrast, no one was killed in a home during the 1971 San Fernando, California, earthquake (magnitude 6.6), which occurred at about 6:00 A.M.. Because of their construction, the houses held together under very severe jolting and, although many were badly damaged, the occupants were unharmed.

During daytime working hours, many people are in offices, factories, and stores, or on the streets, either walking or riding. Their individual experiences and chances for survival in an earthquake depend upon the particular circumstances that exist at the moment the earthquake begins and how they react to those circumstances. If you are in a modern high-rise building, well designed by experienced structural engineers and built of structural steel or reinforced concrete, you are relatively safe even though the structure may vibrate noticeably and suffer some damage. Some buildings are designed to be flexible and are expected to sway back and forth during an earthquake, without danger to the structural integrity of the building. Occupants may not be aware of this basic engineering fact and may become frightened, perhaps foolishly running for the elevators and exits. Electrical power is apt to go out, stopping the elevators and leaving passengers stranded between floors. And because falling objects, such as broken glass and decorative panels, usually land on the sidewalks, people who run out of buildings are often injured. It is much better to stay inside and protect yourself from falling objects or toppled furniture by getting under a desk or table. Remember that well-constructed buildings will sway for as long as a minute in a great earthquake, so condition yourself to remain calm and help others do the same. Panic is a serious hazard during any disaster, but often a few sensible persons can counteract it.

It is unfortunate that not all of our buildings are well constructed. Our cities contain many old buildings that will not survive strong earthquake shaking. Constructed before building codes contained adequate seismic design requirements, most of these old structures are from one to five stories high and are used for offices, apartments, and stores. If the shaking lasts long enough, the worst of them will collapse, as they did in San

This 12-story apartment building in Caracas, Venezuela, collapsed during the 1967 earthquake (magnitude 6.5). (Courtesy of California Division of Mines and Geology)

Fernando in 1971 and in Coalinga in 1983. These earthquakes produced strong shaking for only 10 and 6 seconds, respectively, but that was long enough to shake down many old buildings. Many more would have collapsed if the strong motion had lasted a few seconds longer, because the amount of damage is highly dependent on the duration of the shaking. Each additional cycle of back-and-forth motion results in increased damage to the walls, floors, beams, and columns. As the cracking and breaking progresses, the building becomes weaker and eventually collapses if the shaking lasts long enough.

The most dangerous of these old buildings are those constructed of bricks or concrete blocks without steel reinforcement and with mortar of poor quality. Because they are not well tied together structurally, they quickly fall apart in an earthquake. Sometimes walls fall out, roofs separate from the walls and come down, and parapets fall onto the streets. Obviously, there is a great need to repair and upgrade old buildings of this kind in earthquake regions of the country.

Buildings whose parts are securely tied together fare well in earthquakes, regardless of the materials used in their construction. That is why a wood-frame house is so secure—its walls, floors, and partitions are held together by extensive nailing and bracing. It won't come apart even in violent motion. The same is true of buildings with steel frameworks; the parts are securely tied together with bolts or welding and the structure cannot be shaken apart. Reinforced concrete buildings behave the same way if adequate reinforcing steel is used, especially in columns and at joints where beams and columns meet. The successful performance of a reinforced concrete structure depends not so much upon the sizes of the structural members as upon "details" (as the engineer calls them) of how the reinforcing steel is placed. With proper design and construction, a reinforced concrete structure will hold together tenaciously and protect the occupants from a collapse. Even masonry buildings of bricks and blocks can be properly reinforced to resist earthquake motion.

Owners and developers need to realize these simple facts and must be willing to pay for proper engineering design and construction to ensure a safe structure. The cost of adequate seismic resistance is very low—only a few percent of the building cost—if it is designed into the structure initially, but very high if the building must be upgraded at a later time. In fact, upgrading an existing building can cost almost as much as constructing a new building.

If you live or work in an unsafe building, your chances of being hurt or killed in an earthquake are obviously much higher than they should be. Therefore, it is especially important that you take effective measures to protect yourself when the earthquake comes. If you cannot get under a sturdy table or desk, move to a doorway or a corner of the room and cover your head.

You can perform a valuable service by lending your support to politicians, architects, and engineers who propose local ordinances that require the upgrading of dangerous buildings. Unfortunately, some building owners are unwilling to make their property safe and must be forced to do so by the community.

Other Earthquake Effects

Perhaps you will be riding in a car when an earthquake comes. If the ground shaking is slight, you may not notice it because you will have become accustomed to the ordinary shaking of the vehicle. But if the ground motion is strong, the car will begin to sway noticeably and your natural reaction will be to slow down and stop. People who have been in cars during earthquakes report that it feels like having four flat tires. Try to stop the car away from tall buildings or other structures that might send debris down onto the car. If you are riding in a train, you can only

Sections of the Golden State Freeway (Interstate 5) collapsed in the 1971 San Fernando earthquake. Two people were killed when the overpass in the foreground fell on them. (Photo by R. E. Wallace, courtesy of USGS)

hope that the train slows to a safe stop before encountering any bent rails.

A common fear, often exploited in the movies, is that the ground will swallow you up during an earthquake; in fact, fissures rarely open on the surface. An open field, away from buildings, is the safest place to be.

You can expect roads, pipelines, power lines, and electrical substations to be damaged during earthquakes. Therefore, water supplies, electricity,

Table 1-1

**Expected Losses in the Next Major Earthquake
in the Los Angeles and San Francisco Areas**

Fault Creating the Earthquake	Magnitude of the Earthquake	Deaths	Hospitalized Injuries	Property Damage
Los Angeles and Vicinity				
San Andreas Fault	8.3	3,000 to 12,000	12,000 to 48,000	$20 billion to $50 billion
Newport- Inglewood Fault[a]	7.5	4,000 to 21,000	16,000 to 84,000	$30 billion to $60 billion
San Francisco Bay Area				
San Andreas Fault	8.3	3,000 to 11,000	12,000 to 44,000	$20 billion to $40 billion
Hayward Fault	7.5	1,000 to 3,000	4,000 to 10,000	$5 billion to $20 billion

Note: The number of deaths depends upon time of day and season of the year. The figures given in the table assume no dam failures; a single dam failure could cause many thousands of additional deaths.
[a]This fault caused the 1933 Long Beach earthquake.

phone lines, and sewers may be out of service, and travel may be restricted. You can also expect an overloading of hospital, fire-fighting, and police services.

Earthquake Losses

Even in an earthquake of moderate size, the total losses can be considerable. The 1971 San Fernando earthquake resulted in 58 deaths, many injuries, and over $500 million property damage (1971 dollars), yet its magnitude was only 6.6. In a great earthquake the losses can be staggering. It is reliably estimated that a repetition of the 1906 San Francisco earthquake would cause from 3,000 to 11,000 deaths (depending upon the season and the time of day) and billions of dollars in property damage. Loss estimates for both the Los Angeles and San Francisco regions are given in Table 1-1.

Considered in a worldwide context, however, the United States has an excellent record for avoiding loss of life in earthquakes. Whereas an average of 10,000 people are killed each year by earthquakes throughout the world, the U.S. has suffered only about 1,500 earthquake-related deaths in the more than 80 years since 1900. During this same period, there have been over 40 earthquakes with magnitudes of 6.0 or greater in the conterminous United States. At least that many have also occurred in Alaska, eight of which had a magnitude greater than 8.0. Most Alaskan earthquakes have occurred in remote areas and have caused little loss of life and only minor damage to man-made structures. The great Alaskan earthquake of 1964 (magnitude 8.4) was a tragic exception: it caused 131 deaths.

In other parts of the world—especially Central and South America, the Mediterranean region, and Asia—the figures tell a different story. Thousands of people die even in moderate-size earthquakes. Here are some figures for strong earthquakes: In Iran in 1981, 15,000 died in a 7.7 magnitude earthquake, and in 1981, 3,000 more died in a 6.9 magnitude earthquake. In Italy in 1980, 3,100 people died in a magnitude 7.0 earthquake. In Algeria in 1980, about 5,000 died in the magnitude 7.3 El Asnam earthquake. The year 1976 was particularly devastating: The Tangshan, China, earthquake (magnitude 7.8) took a quarter of a million lives (almost 25 percent of the city's population); the Guatemala earthquake (magnitude 7.5), 23,000; the New Guinea earthquake (magnitude 7.1), 6,000; the Philippines earthquake (magnitude 8.0), 6,500; and the eastern Turkey earthquake (magnitude 7.3), 5,000 lives.*

* See Table A-2, Significant Earthquakes of the World, p. 174.

This fence in Marin County was offset 8.5 feet during the 1906 San Francisco earthquake. The San Andreas fault runs left to right across the field at the spot where the fence is broken. During the earthquake, the land on the far side of the fault moved to the right, carrying the fence with it. (Photo by G. K. Gilbert, courtesy of USGS)

2

Why Do We Have Earthquakes?

The earth-ox changes his burden to the other shoulder.
—Ancient Chinese proverb

SURELY MAN HAS ASKED "WHY?" since he first felt the earth tremble beneath his feet. People have always been frightened by earthquakes, and each culture developed its own superstitious beliefs to explain them. According to an ancient Japanese legend, the islands of Japan rested on the back of a giant catfish whose movements caused the earth to shake. The Algonquin Indians of North America said that a giant tortoise supported the earth, which shook whenever the tortoise shifted from one foot to another. In parts of Asia, a frog was the culprit; in India, a giant mole; and in China, an ox supported the earth.

Early Explanations

Aristotle turned to the inside of the earth to find the causes of earthquakes. He theorized that the winds of the atmosphere were drawn into the earth, which was filled with caverns and passageways. The winds, he believed, were agitated by fire and moved about trying to escape, thus causing earthquakes and sometimes erupting as volcanoes. His views held sway for many centuries even though he offered no basis for his conjectures, simply drawing on his fertile imagination. Aristotle is also responsible for the still-prevalent notion of "earthquake weather." He said that when air was drawn into the earth prior to an earthquake, the air above the earth became calmer and thinner, making it hard to breathe. Four hundred years later, Pliny wrote: "Tremors of the earth never occur except when the sea is calm and the sky so still that birds are unable to soar because all the breath that carries them has been withdrawn." Because

In this painting from the Edo period, the common people are trying to subdue the catfish whose movements, according to legend, caused earthquakes. (Courtesy of K. Ishida)

such conditions are often present in hot, humid weather, such weather became known as earthquake weather and presumably signaled the coming of an earthquake.

Earthquakes were often interpreted as punishments meted out by angry gods. In Greek mythology, Poseidon, ruler of the sea, caused earthquakes when he was angry. His counterpart in Roman legends was Neptune, who not only could strike fear into men with earthquakes but also could bring floods over the land and waves onto the shore. In eighteenth-century Europe, clergymen also tended to take a moralistic view of earthquakes. One could read in a London journal of 1752: "Earthquakes generally happen to great cities and towns. The chastening rod is directed where there are inhabitants, the objects of its monition, not to bare cliffs and uninhabited beach." The famous Lisbon earthquake of 1755 occurred on All Saints' Day at a time when people were in church. There was great loss of life from a sequence of several shocks and a giant tsunami that devastated the waterfront. To make matters worse, fires subsequently burned through the entire city. Those who believed in God's retribution for sinful behavior felt vindicated. One Portuguese nun reported that she had a vision from Jesus Christ warning that the city would be punished for its wickedness. A clergyman in England chastised the people of Lisbon for their "lewdness and debauchery," while others blamed the dreadful Inquisition and noted that the Palace of the Inquisition was one of the first buildings to be destroyed.

Crustal Plates and Earthquakes

Today we have the advantage of many years of geologic detective work that has produced a remarkably clear picture of the structure of the earth and the causes of earthquakes. The causes can be readily understood once we recognize the dynamic character of the earth and the changes that are slowly taking place in the earth's crust. The crust is relatively thin and covers the earth to a depth of from 70 kilometers (about 40 miles) under the oceans to 150 kilometers (about 90 miles) under the continents.* That the crust is indeed thin can be seen from the following comparison: If the earth were reduced to the size of an egg, the solid crust would be as thin as the eggshell. However, the crust is not in one piece but is broken into a number of large fragments, called *plates*. The map (Figure 2-1) shows the outline of these plates, which vary in width from a few hundred to many thousands of kilometers.

Beneath the crust forces are at work that cause the plates to move, usually at a rate of a few centimeters† per year. The origin of these forces deep within the earth is not clear, but they may be caused by slowly moving currents in the hot molten interior, the currents themselves being produced by thermal convection and the dynamic effects from the rotation of the earth. In some regions the plates are being driven apart as new crustal material is forced upward from the earth's interior (for example, this happens along the Mid-Atlantic ridge); in other places, the plates slide past one another (such as along the San Andreas fault in California); and in still other places, called *subduction zones*, they push directly against each other (for example, off the western coasts of South and Central America, off the coast of Alaska, and off the coast of Japan). The difference in motion between the plates, irrespective of its direction, causes the rocks to fracture, thus creating an earthquake.

It is not surprising, therefore, that most earthquakes (almost 95 percent of them) occur at the edges of plates. This fact is apparent when you compare the map of the plates (Figure 2-1) with the map showing the major seismic zones of the world (centerfold). Earthquakes produced by plate movement are called *tectonic earthquakes*. Although they usually occur at plate boundaries, a small percent occur in the interiors of the plates. A few other earthquakes, such as those in Hawaii, are volcanic in origin, and even fewer are caused by human activities (filling of reservoirs, pumping into wells, mining, and large explosions).

* One kilometer equals approximately 5/8 of a mile; to obtain miles, multiply the number of kilometers by 5/8 (or 0.62).
† One centimeter equals approximately 4/10 of an inch; to obtain inches, multiply the number of centimeters by 0.4.

The zone of earthquakes surrounding the Pacific Ocean is known as the Circum-Pacific belt; about 90 percent of the world's earthquakes occur there. The next most seismic region, accounting for 5 or 6 percent of the earthquakes, is the Alpide belt, the zone that extends from the Mediter-

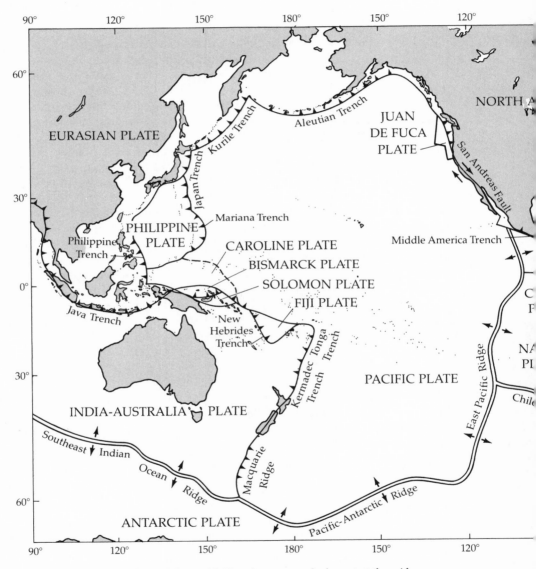

Figure 2-1. Crustal plates of the world. The plates are pushed apart at the mid-ocean ridges by the intrusion of magma from the mantle; the process is known as seafloor

ranean region eastward through Turkey, Iran, and northern India. The remaining 4 or 5 percent of earthquakes occur along the mid-ocean ridges and in the interiors of plates.

Our knowledge of the causes of earthquakes has greatly expanded in

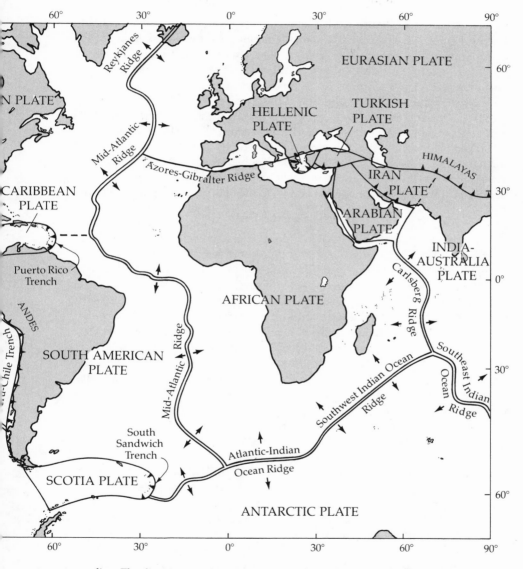

spreading. The directions of plate movement are shown by arrows. Subduction zones are marked on the plate boundaries by the symbol ▲▲. Most tsunamis originate in these zones.

the last century. Before 1900, scientists didn't even have accurate information as to where earthquakes were located or at what depths; that information had to await the development of the seismograph, the instrument that made it possible to systematically record and locate earthquakes. So it is no wonder that people of earlier times found it necessary to invent imaginative stories to explain earthquakes. Without precise mapping techniques, using laser beams and satellite photographs, they had no way of knowing that the crust is constantly changing in form and that entire continents are moving slowly. Without the technology to remove a sample of rock from the bottom of the sea and determine its composition, age, and magnetic characteristics, they could not know about the intrusion of magma into the seafloor at the Mid-Atlantic ridge (thereby creating new crust and forcing the plates to move). Without numerous other scientific and engineering developments of the last century, it would have been impossible to obtain the complete picture of the earth's structure and formation we have today. Seismologists, geologists, oceanographers, surveyors, biologists, anthropologists, archeologists, and electronics engineers have contributed their specialized talents to the task of creating this picture.

Structure of the Earth

The principal parts of the earth are the crust, mantle, outer core, and inner core. The crust is the solid and more-or-less rigid layer at the outer surface. Known scientifically as the lithosphere, the crust is broken up into the slowly moving plates already described. The mantle, which is beneath the crust, is composed of rock in the molten state; the red-hot lava that pours out of volcanoes comes from the mantle. As we go toward the center of the earth, the temperature, pressure, and density increase. At the center the temperature is about 4200° C (for comparison, steel melts at 1500° C), the pressure is 3.6 million times atmospheric pressure, and the density is 13 times greater than the density of water (for comparison, ordinary iron has a density about 7.9 times that of water). The inner core behaves like a solid but the outer core behaves more like a viscous liquid. Most of what we know about the interior of the earth comes from studies of the travel of waves generated by earthquakes.

The solid crust, the oceans, and even the air we breathe were formed from materials in the mantle that rose to the surface and cooled a long time ago. This process is continuing today and is evident whenever lava emerges from the earth. Lava solidifies into rock, thus adding to the crust, and gives off water vapor and gases that contribute to the oceans and the atmosphere. Beneath the crustal plates, in the outermost part of the mantle, is a thin layer of hot, molten viscous material, called the asthenosphere, over which the plates slide. In certain places, such as the Mid-Atlantic ridge, molten material from the asthenosphere is pushed up into the litho-

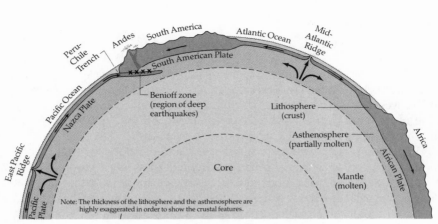

Figure 2-2. Cross section of the earth's crust. New crust is formed at the Mid-Atlantic ridge and at the East Pacific ridge. The Nazca and South American plates collide at the Peru-Chile trench, where the Nazca plate subducts beneath the continent. Deep earthquakes occur along the inclined contact zone (Benioff zone). Subduction not only produces the deep trench but also pushes up the Andes and creates volcanoes.

sphere, where it cools and forms new crust. This process pushes apart the South American and African plates as well as the North American and Eurasian plates. The average rate at which these plates are separating is about 7 centimeters per year (almost 3 inches), which means that the Atlantic Ocean is widening every year by that amount.*

The process just described, known as *seafloor spreading,* occurs not only at the Mid-Atlantic ridge but also at all of the mid-ocean ridges shown on the map of the crustal plates (Figure 2-1). For instance, at the East-Pacific ridge, new crust is being created that results in spreading of the Pacific and Nazca plates. Because of the spreading process, the slowly moving plates collide with one another in other locations; at these collision zones, they push up mountain ranges and create volcanoes and islands, not to mention earthquakes.

Thus we see that the earth is not static but dynamic, with its topography constantly undergoing change. If it were not so, the earth would long ago have developed a flat surface due to erosion and the oceans would be spread uniformly over the earth.

Subduction Zones

The manner in which the plates collide varies from one location to another. Along the western coast of South America, the Nazca plate and the South American plate meet in a direct head-on confrontation. Clearly, one must yield to the other. It so happens that the Nazca plate has been deflected downward beneath the South American plate in a process known

* Putting it in more familiar terms, the distance from New York to London will increase by 23 feet in the next 100 years.

as *subduction*. Just as new crust is being formed from the mantle at the mid-ocean ridges, so also is old crust being returned to the mantle at the subduction zones. In a sense, the entire earth is being recycled. The principal subduction zones are located along the Aleutian Islands, near Japan, in the western Pacific Ocean (near the Philippines), in Indonesia, at the base of the Himalayas, north of New Zealand, off the western coasts of South and Central America, and in the Persian Gulf.

When one plate is subducted under another, earthquakes occur along the inclined contact surface, called the Benioff zone (after Hugo Benioff, a Caltech seismologist). Consequently, some earthquakes occur at great depths; furthermore, those at the greatest depths are located farthest inland wherever the oceanic plate is going under the continental plate (as along the South American coast; see Figure 2-2). Earthquakes with depths as great as 700 kilometers (over 400 miles) have occurred in subduction zones.

Deep ocean trenches are another feature of subduction zones. The Peru-Chile trench reaches a maximum depth of 8,063 meters* (about 5 miles) below sea level only 100 kilometers (60 miles) from the coast line. Other trenches formed by the process of subduction are the Aleutian trench, Japan trench, Java trench, Middle America trench, and several more around the edges of the Pacific plate. The deepest spot in the ocean is the Challenger Deep, located at the southern end of the Mariana trench (depth 10,915 meters, almost 7 miles) and named for the research ship that discovered the trench in the 1870s.

Volcanic chains are also typical of subduction zones. As one plate is being subducted under another, it tends to push upward against the overlying plate, thus creating mountain ranges and volcanoes. Sometimes the volcanoes are part of a continent, as in the Andes, and in other places they form a chain of islands, as in the Aleutians and some parts of the western Pacific Ocean. The Himalayas are also created by subduction, being formed by pressures from the India-Australia plate pushing northward and subducting under the Eurasian plate.

But there is even more to the subduction story. Most of the world's tsunamis are generated by vertical movement of the seafloor in subduction zones, a process that is explained in detail in Chapter 4. For instance, the eastern coasts of Japan have been subjected to many large tsunamis that originated in the Japan trench, where the Pacific plate is being subducted under the Eurasian plate.

The San Andreas Fault

The plate boundaries in some regions of the world are sliding past one another instead of colliding at subduction zones or separating at ocean

---

* One meter equals approximately 3.3 feet; to obtain feet, multiply the number of meters by 3.3.

Wallace Creek in central California flows across the San Andreas fault, adapting its course as each earthquake causes the North American plate (top) to move to the right and the Pacific plate (bottom) to the left. After hundreds of years of earthquakes, the stream is offset by 400 feet. Smaller and more recent offsets are visible at the right. (Photo by R. E. Wallace, courtesy of USGS)

ridges. The best known of these regions is the San Andreas fault zone, a plate boundary along the western coast of the United States that extends southward through the Sea of Cortez (see Figure 2-1 and Figure 8-1). At this particular boundary the Pacific plate is moving northwest past the North American plate. Relative movement between the plates is 5 to 8 centimeters per year. Although this amount of movement occurs steadily between the main bodies of the plates, slippage along the fault zone occurs erratically. When the strength of the rocks is overcome in a particular reach of the fault, the rocks break and slippage occurs. Sometimes a short length of fault ruptures and a small earthquake occurs; other times, the rupture is hundreds of kilometers long and a great earthquake shakes the western coast. In the 1906 San Francisco and 1857 Fort Tejon earthquakes, the rupture lengths were over 400 kilometers (250 miles). Earthquakes on the San Andreas fault typically occur at relatively shallow depths of 5 to 40 kilometers below the surface.

The 1886 Charleston, South Carolina, earthquake that collapsed these buildings killed 110 people and injured scores. Earthquakes of this severity (estimated magnitude 7.0) are rare in the eastern United States. (Photo by J. K. Hillers, courtesy of USGS)

Intraplate Earthquakes

Earthquakes in the interiors of plates, called *intraplate earthquakes*, occur occasionally throughout the world. Most likely they are caused by the build-up of strains from pressures developed at the plate boundaries. For instance, China is being squeezed in two directions, from the east by the Pacific plate and from the south by the India-Australia plate. Presumably, these pressures are responsible for the earthquakes that occur throughout the country, including the 1976 Tangshan earthquake that resulted in such a huge loss of life. Examples of large intraplate earthquakes in the United States are the New Madrid earthquakes of 1811 and 1812 in the Mississippi River valley and the Charleston, South Carolina, earthquake of 1886.

The Hawaiian Islands

The Hawaiian Archipelago, a chain of islands extending in a straight line for 3,000 kilometers (almost 2,000 miles), is also the result of plate movement. A local "hot spot" beneath the crustal plate pushes molten material to the surface, creating a volcanic island. As the Pacific plate moves toward the northwest, the hot spot remains fixed in position in the mantle; thus, the island chain appears to grow toward the southeast. The newest island, Hawaii, is at the southeastern end of the chain and is currently volcanically active; older islands extend in succession toward the northwest. Kauai is the oldest of the main islands familiar to tourists, but the archipelago extends to Midway Island and beyond. Midway is about 25,000,000 years old and about 2,400 kilometers (1,500 miles) from the island of Hawaii, which indicates an average rate of plate movement of 10 centimeters per year. Earthquakes associated with volcanic activity on the island of Hawaii are small but very common.

The 1976 Guatemala Earthquake

A classic example of an earthquake caused by plate movement took place in Central America in 1976. Guatemala is literally cut in two because it straddles the boundary between the North American and Caribbean plates (Figure 2-1). Along this boundary the Motagua fault runs for 300 kilometers (about 200 miles), from the Caribbean Sea on the east to the mountains west of Guatemala City. It was slippage on this fault that killed 23,000 people in the terrible earthquake of February 4, 1976.

Pressures from the East Pacific ridge are pushing the Cocos plate eastward against the Caribbean plate (Figure 2-1). The Cocos plate is subducted downward and goes back into the mantle, creating the Middle America trench, which reaches a depth of 6,662 meters (about 4 miles) below sea level. This subduction process has produced a long chain of volcanoes that stretches along the western side of Central America from Panama to Mexico. Even as the Cocos plate is being pushed eastward against the Caribbean plate, the Mid-Atlantic ridge is creating a westward pressure against the North American plate. The result is relative movement along the boundary between the Caribbean and North American plates, with the former moving east and the latter west.

The Motagua fault in Guatemala is part of this plate boundary. The relative movement between the plates—about 2 meters every 100 years—is responsible for Guatemala's long history of damaging earthquakes. The 1976 earthquake, magnitude 7.5, resulted in a maximum ground displacement of about 1.3 meters near the epicenter. The strong ground shaking lasted for about 30 seconds.

Damage from the earthquake was extensive in dozens of rural villages, where adobe-type construction is common. In some, such as El Progreso in the middle of the country, hardly a building was left standing. The survivors were isolated by blocked highways and collapsed bridges. Telephone lines were down, and all electricity was out. Rescue and relief work was further hampered by thousands of landslides on the steep hillsides, which are composed of soft rock. Even in Guatemala City, the capital, some of the newer buildings were heavily damaged.

Because the communication links between the capital and the rural villages were destroyed, the severity of the damage and the extent of the death toll were not immediately recognized. On February 5, the day after the earthquake, the wire services reported that 2,000 people were believed

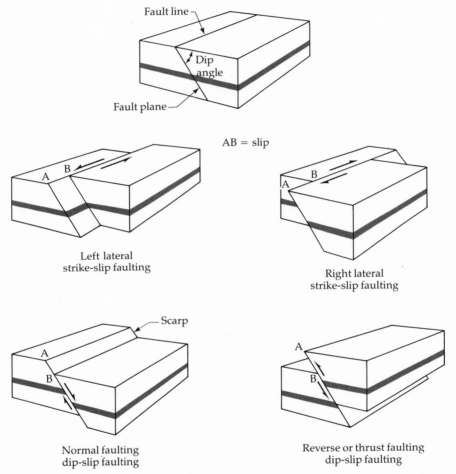

Figure 2-3. Types of fault movement. In strike-slip faulting, the crustal blocks move horizontally; in dip-slip faulting, they move vertically. Horizontal movement may be left lateral (as along the Motagua fault in Guatemala) or right lateral (as along the San Andreas fault). Vertical movement may be normal or reverse, depending upon whether the lower block moves up or down with respect to the upper block.

killed. By the next day, as more information became available, they reported 4,000 deaths and 12,000 hurt; on the third day, newspaper headlines were saying 5,000 deaths. Five days after the earthquake, newspapers in the United States reported 15,000 deaths and 40,000 injuries. Eventually, it became known that 23,000 died, 77,000 were injured, and more than a million people were made homeless.

Types of Fault Movement

Slippage along the Motagua fault in Guatemala was of a type known as left-lateral movement. This means that the plates move horizontally past one another with the land mass on the far side of the fault (that is, the side away from the observer) moving to the left. By contrast, earth movement along the San Andreas fault is right lateral. Faults which move horizontally are called strike-slip faults because they slip along the strike of the fault. The strike is the direction of the horizontal line where the fault plane intersects the surface, and the slip is the amount of displacement (distance *AB* in Figure 2-3).

Some faults move primarily in the vertical direction, leaving a steep exposed face called a *scarp*. If the hanging wall, that is, the upper block

The upward movement of the crustal block on the left created this large fault scarp during the December 1954 Fairview Peak earthquake in Nevada. (Photo by K. V. Steinbrugge, courtesy of USGS)

During the Idaho earthquake of October 28, 1983 (magnitude 6.9), the ground dropped over a meter, leaving two facing scarps and creating a graben (German for grave). Surface faulting was visible for about 28 miles. (Photo by R. E. Wallace, courtesy of USGS)

of rock, moves downward, it is called normal faulting; if upward, reverse or thrust faulting. Vertical faulting is also known as dip-slip faulting because movement is along the dip of the fault (the angle between the plane of the fault and the horizontal). Again, the slip is the distance *AB* in Figure 2-3. Of course, many combinations of horizontal and vertical slippage are possible. For instance, a left-lateral reverse fault means that the hanging wall moves upward and to the right in comparison with the foot wall.

Reservoirs Can Trigger Earthquakes

In several places around the world earthquakes have been created by the filling of large reservoirs. One of the earliest recorded instances took place when Hoover Dam on the Colorado River was completed and Lake Mead began to fill. Prior to construction of the dam, the region around Lake Mead was not known to have any seismic activity. After the lake began filling in 1935, earthquakes occurred. The first ones were noticed in 1936 and the largest one (magnitude 5.0) occurred in 1939 when the lake was about 80 percent full. The maximum lake level was reached in 1941, and low-level seismic activity has continued since that time, with felt earthquakes occurring occasionally.

The largest reservoir-induced earthquake took place at Koyna Dam, near Bombay, India; this dam was also constructed in a nonseismic zone. However, soon after the reservoir began to fill in 1962, small earthquakes were felt. The reservoir was full by 1965, and in 1967 several significant earthquakes occurred. The largest, on December 11, had a magnitude of 6.4 and resulted in extensive damage to a nearby village, 177 deaths, and 2,300 injuries. After that, the earthquake activity decreased and finally appears to have stopped.

Events similar to those at Hoover and Koyna Dams have occurred in China (Hsinfengkiang Dam), France (Monteynard Dam), Zimbabwe-Rhodesia (Kariba Dam), Greece (Kremasta Dam), California (Oroville Dam), Egypt (Aswan High Dam), and a few other places. While reservoir-induced earthquakes usually are small in size, several have had magnitudes between 5.0 and 6.0, and three have had magnitudes greater than 6.0.

How can a reservoir trigger an earthquake? To answer this question, we note that the filling of a reservoir has three principal effects on the earth beneath it. First, the weight of the water places a load on the earth, thereby creating additional stresses in the underlying soil and rock. Second, these additional stresses cause an increase in pore-water pressure in those parts of the soil and rock which contained water before the impounding of the reservoir took place. And third, water from the reservoir flows into the underlying material, increasing its water content and filling cracks and pores. Any or all of these effects can result in earthquakes: the increased stresses in the rocks can trigger an earthquake on a fault that was nearly at the point of slippage; the increased pore-water pressure can decrease the strength of a rock formation by reducing the contact pressure between grains or particles; and the increase in water content can have a "lubricating" effect by reducing friction along fault planes and fracture planes. Note that the reservoir is not the principal cause of an earthquake, but it can trigger an earthquake by causing the strain to be released sooner than otherwise.

As an interesting sidelight, it has been found in a few locations that too rapid draining of a reservoir also can produce seismic activity. This happens when the water pressure at the bottom of the reservoir decreases more rapidly (because of the rapid drawing down of the water level) than the pore-water pressures within the rocks can be relieved. The pore-water pressure can be reduced only at a relatively slow rate, because it takes time for the water to find its way out of the rocks. The consequence is that interior pressures exist in the rocks and cause them to be weakened, resulting in earthquake activity. Nurek Reservoir in Tadzhikistan, a province located in the southern part of the Soviet Union just north of the Afghanistan border, is so sensitive that measurable seismic activity begins immediately after the water level is lowered by as little as 3 meters.

And So Can Pumping into Wells

This phenomenon was first noted at the Rocky Mountain Arsenal, located northeast of Denver, Colorado, on the outskirts of the city. A hole about 3 kilometers deep was drilled for the purpose of disposing of contaminated water. The waste water was pumped into the hole beginning in 1962, and almost immediately earthquakes began to occur. Pumping continued at various rates for the next four years but was discontinued when it became evident that the number of earthquakes was closely related to the amount of fluid injected into the earth. The earthquake hypocenters were within a few kilometers of the hole and at very shallow depths (5 kilometers, or 3 miles) in an area not previously known for its seismicity. The earthquakes were felt by the residents of Denver and caused great concern. Most of the earthquakes were small, with magnitudes less than 4.0, but the largest had a magnitude of 5.2 and occurred in 1967, about a year after pumping was stopped. The most likely cause of these earthquakes was the increased pore-water pressure produced in the rocks by the pumping.

An opportunity to verify this conjecture came a few years later near Rangely, a small city in northwestern Colorado. Oil production at the Rangely oil field began in 1945; the oil was taken from a sandstone formation about 1.5 kilometers below the surface. Fluid pressure in the rocks decreased due to the oil removal until 1957, at which time water was pumped back into the wells to facilitate secondary recovery of oil. Pore-water pressures due to this pumping were greater than those in the oil field before the oil was removed. Beginning in 1969, several controlled experiments were performed by the U.S. Geological Survey. Water was pumped into and out of the wells, and the pore-water pressures were measured. In addition, seismographs were installed to measure any earthquakes. It was found that small earthquakes (magnitudes 3.5 or less) were occurring frequently in the injection zone and that the amount of seismic activity could be correlated with the pumping. When injection took place and pore pressure increased, the number of earthquakes increased; when water was pumped out, the number decreased. Thus, the relationship between pore-water pressures and earthquakes was established. Whether or not pumping of water into wells or cavities could be used as a practical scheme for controlling large earthquakes is still a subject for speculation. Obvious difficulties include controlling the size of the earthquakes and dealing with legal problems that would result from "acts of man" rather than "acts of God."

Charles Darwin and Plate Tectonics

During the voyage of the *Beagle*, Charles Darwin studied the rocks and sea life along the coast of Chile. He observed the presence of sea shells embedded in the rocks hundreds of feet above sea level. One February day in 1835 he was on shore, lying in the woods to rest, when he felt a large earthquake. "It came on suddenly, and lasted two minutes, but the time appeared much longer," he wrote. He reported that a great wave approached the shore, tearing up trees and cottages when it struck. Ships were carried far up on the land.

Upon closer investigation of the shoreline, he saw from the sea life that the ground had been raised up during the earthquake. "There can be no doubt that the land round the bay of Concepción was upraised two or three feet. . . . At the Island of Santa Maria the elevation was greater. . . ." Although he had no knowledge of plate tectonics nor of the structure of the earth, he now had a clue as to how the sea shells came to be so high up in the mountains. "At Valparaiso . . . shells are found at the height of 1300 feet; it is hardly possible to doubt that this great elevation has been effected by successive small uprisings, such as that which accompanied or caused the earthquake of this year . . . ." He may have anticipated modern theories of plate tectonics when he wrote, "A bad earthquake at once destroys our oldest associations: the earth, the very emblem of solidity, has moved beneath our feet like a thin crust over a fluid."

(Courtesy of the Bettman Archive)

The south wing of Government Hill School in Anchorage, Alaska, was split in two by a massive land-slide during the 1964 earthquake. The earth apparently shifted slowly as desks and equipment remained upright. (Photo by M. G. Bonilla, courtesy of USGS)

3

Landslides, Liquefaction, and Other Earthquake Hazards

It is a bitter and humiliating thing to see works, which have cost man so much time and labor, overthrown in one minute.
—Charles Darwin, *The Voyage of the Beagle*
(on the 1835 Chile earthquake)

AS THE FIGURES MOUNT in the hours and days following an earthquake—gradually accounting for the dead, the missing, and the homeless—we are shocked but not surprised, because we know that earthquakes have the capacity to cause death, damage, and destruction on a huge scale. The actual shaking of the earth accounts for only part of the losses. Earthquakes produce other geological effects, such as landslides and liquefaction, that kill people and animals, ravage the land, and destroy buildings. An earthquake may even create a tsunami that travels across the ocean to wreak havoc in a coastal city thousands of miles away.

Seismologists classify earthquake *hazards*—those destructive events caused by earthquakes—as natural (for example, landslides) or as man-made (such as flooding from the collapse of a dam). We have listed the principal hazards in Table 3-1. Some of these hazards are described in detail in this chapter; others are discussed throughout the book.

Landslides at Mount Huascarán and Lituya Bay

Because Peru lies above the subduction zone where the Nazca plate is being pushed beneath the South American plate, it suffers repeatedly from the effects of earthquakes. None had more horrifying effects than the May 31, 1970, earthquake that originated beneath the Pacific Ocean about 25

A landslide originating high on the slopes of Mt. Huascarán in Peru buried the city of Yungay and its 18,000 inhabitants. The slide was caused by an earthquake off the coast, about 80 miles away. Cemetery Hill, in the lower right corner, was the only part of the city that was spared. The main cathedral and city plaza are now covered by 30 feet of mud and debris; only the tops of a few palm trees in the center of the flow mark their position. The slide that covered Yungay was only a small branch of the main slide which traveled to the right down the canyon on the other side of the ridge just above the city. (Photo by George Plafker, courtesy of USGS)

Lituya Bay, Alaska, after the 1958 earthquake. The slide came down the mountainside (A) into the north arm of the bay, and washed 900 feet up the mountain on the near side (B). The slide-generated wave scoured the mountainside and shoreline clean. A fishing boat was carried over the spit (C) and dumped into the ocean. (Courtesy of NOAA/EDIS)

kilometers off the coast near the city of Chimbote. High up on the side of Mount Huascarán, about 130 kilometers (80 miles) from the source of the earthquake, the shaking loosened rocks and ice and a gigantic landslide began. Gathering speed and mass as it rushed down the mountain, the slide quickly assumed tremendous proportions. It sped at over 200 kilometers per hour (120 miles per hour) down a long valley, filling it with rock, ice, and mud, and partially destroying the town of Ranrahirca, located about 12 kilometers below the mountain. Part of the landslide branched off to one side, swept over a high ridge, and roared through the village of Yungay. The village was obliterated; only a few of its inhabitants were able to escape by running to higher ground as the landslide approached. One survivor likened the oncoming slide to a gigantic breaker coming in from the ocean with a deafening roar and rumble—it was, in fact, over 30 meters (100 feet) high.

In these two towns alone, over 18,000 people were buried; a total of perhaps 25,000 people were killed by this single landslide. Elsewhere in the region, numerous smaller slides and the destruction of thousands of adobe-type buildings accounted for even more deaths. The final toll was 67,000 dead and 800,000 homeless—the greatest seismic disaster in the Western Hemisphere.

Far to the north, in a region vastly different in climate and population, lies Lituya Bay, in Glacier Bay National Park, Alaska. A narrow inlet connects Lituya Bay with the open waters of the Gulf of Alaska. The head of the bay is along the Fairweather fault, a major earthquake fault that parallels the coastline. The fault has created two arms, one going northwest and the other southeast, at the head of the bay. Here, too, an earthquake precipitated a landslide, but with very different effects.

On July 9, 1958, a large earthquake on the Fairweather fault set off a landslide on the side of the mountain above Lituya Bay. A huge mass of rock and soil rushed downward, denuding the mountainside and exposing the base rock beneath. The moving mass crashed into the northern arm of the bay, rushed across it, and still had enough momentum to carry the slide material up the mountain on the opposite side, scraping the mountain clean of its forest cover to a height of over 300 meters (900 feet). The slide created a huge water wave that swept down Lituya Bay toward the ocean— a wave so high that it washed completely over the spits at the mouth of the bay.

Lituya Bay is a favorite site for fishing boats, and three were in the bay when the wave came. One, with Bill and Vi Swanson aboard, was carried high above the normal water surface, transported completely over one of the spits, and dropped into the ocean. The boat sank but miraculously the Swansons survived and were rescued from the sea two hours later. During their nightmarish ride on the giant wave, their boat was pummeled by trees and debris. At one point, as they were carried over the spit, they could see standing trees *below* them. Of the two other boats, one survived the wave but the other was sunk and its occupants lost. The skipper of the second surviving boat estimated the wave height at 30 meters.

Other Earthquake Slides

Although gigantic landslides such as those at Mount Huascarán and Lituya Bay occur only occasionally, damaging landslides frequently accompany earthquakes. If you visit Earthquake Lake on the Madison River in Montana, just west of Yellowstone National Park, you will see the remains of a large landslide that dammed the river and created the lake. On August 17, 1959, an earthquake started a slide on a mountain above the river. The slide came down the side of the mountain and swept over a campground, burying forever a number of campers with their tents and vehicles. Then it rushed into the river, completely filling it, and continued up the mountain slope on the far side. The flow of the river was stopped by this natural dam until the new lake was filled.

A huge landslide created a natural dam across the Madison River in Montana, just west of Yellowstone National Park, during the 1959 earthquake. Top: Looking downstream at the dam. The newly created lake is slowly filling and covering the trees. Bottom: Looking upstream at the new dam. The lake is on the far side, and the river bed is now dry. (Top photo by R. W. Bayley, courtesy of USGS; bottom photo courtesy of U.S. Forest Service)

The 1971 earthquake at San Fernando, California, caused hundreds of small landslides in the San Gabriel mountains, damaging roads, homes, and small buildings. In Guatemala, during the 1976 earthquake, thousands of slides came down the hills west and north of Guatemala City. Blocked roads cut off access to many villages and seriously interfered with rescue operations. In the city itself, several new homes on steep hills were swept down the slopes.

The seriousness of the landslide hazard became all too evident to residents of the San Francisco Bay Area in recent rainy seasons, when slides caused by saturated ground did considerable damage to hillsides, houses, and highways. Several people were killed by slides, and two main highways were blocked, one for many weeks. If such sliding can occur *without* an earthquake, imagine the extent of sliding that will result when there *is* an earthquake, especially during the rainy season.

Ground that has been badly weakened by thousands of years of faulting is especially susceptible to slides. In Daly City, a suburban community adjacent to San Francisco, a large housing development is located on the San Andreas fault at the spot where the fault passes into the Pacific Ocean. Even though there has been no significant fault movement in recent years, landsliding occurs frequently along the oceanfront cliffs. The slide area has slowly enlarged, and several houses have already been removed. The process is continuing, and the remaining houses at the edge of the slide are now showing cracks. In this same location, the San Andreas fault was offset several feet during the 1906 earthquake. We can only assume that the people living there were unaware of this danger when they bought their homes. It is surprising that zoning or planning agencies permitted building at so susceptible a site.

Today it is possible to obtain maps of many parts of California showing the areas that are prone to landslides. Developers should consult these maps and investigate the landslide possibilities before constructing any buildings in such areas. If the likelihood of slides is sufficiently great, corrective measures to stabilize the slopes can be taken; even though expensive, such measures may be cheaper than doing repair work later on. If adequate precautions cannot be taken, the site should be left undeveloped.

Landslide and Liquefaction at Turnagain Heights

The most spectacular landslide of the last two decades was caused by a phenomenon known as *liquefaction*, a process in which the soil change. from a firm material into a viscous semi-liquid material that resembles quicksand. Liquefaction occurs when certain types of soils are vibrated, and therefore it is common during earthquakes. When a soil layer liquefies and begins to flow, it can no longer support the weight of any soil or

Liquefaction, a result of the March 27, 1964, Anchorage, Alaska, earthquake, produced a landslide in Turnagain Heights that tore up both earth and houses, moving some as much as 300 feet. (Courtesy of USGS)

structures above it, so landsliding begins and damage occurs. For liquefaction to take place, the soil layer must consist of a suitable material (usually sand) and must be saturated with water. Also, the vibrations from the earthquake must have the proper frequencies, and the shaking must last for a sufficient length of time, usually 10 to 20 seconds.

The necessary conditions for liquefaction existed at Turnagain Heights, a beautiful residential area on a slope overlooking the Knik Arm of Cook Inlet in Anchorage, Alaska. A layer of sandy soil beneath the surface liquefied during the 1964 Good Friday earthquake. With its supporting soil weakened, the hillside slumped downward and slid toward the sea. The ground broke into large chunks that turned and twisted as they moved along; large cracks and fissures appeared between the blocks of earth, and scarps as high as 15 meters were formed. Houses, their occupants still inside, traveled with the earth, twisting and turning and breaking up as they went. The area that slid was 2 kilometers long and averaged about 300 meters in width. Over 70 buildings were dislodged and destroyed by the slide.

Mrs. Lowell Thomas, Jr., whose home was one of those destroyed, wrote a dramatic personal account of her family's experiences for *National Geographic Magazine* (July 1964). They first heard a loud rumble, and then

These Turnagain Heights, Alaska, homes illustrate the destructive capabilities of a land-slide. (Courtesy of NOAA/EDIS)

their house began to shake violently. They rushed outdoors, only to be shaken so severely that they were thrown to the ground, where they lay in the snow for what "seemed an eternity." Then the house began to tear apart, trees crashed to the ground, and the earth split open in huge chunks. The noise was deafening. The earth slid as it was breaking up, carrying them along in a violent and rocking ride. When it finally ended, their house was strewn over 200 meters but their family was alive and uninjured. Not all of their neighbors fared so well; two children who lived next door were buried by the slide.

This same earthquake produced many other slides and spectacular ground failures. In Anchorage, slides at Fourth Avenue, L Street, and Government Hill, all caused by liquefaction, did much damage to build-ings. At Valdez, a submarine landslide, also caused by liquefaction, took away the waterfront facilities when a section of the harbor 60 meters wide and over a kilometer long slid into the sea.

Other Liquefaction Disasters

Spectacular landslides are not the only effects of liquefaction. In June of 1964 an earthquake of magnitude 7.5 took place near Niigata, Japan, in a coastal region with much sandy and thoroughly saturated soil. Liq-uefaction resulted in extensive settlement of the land and damaged roads, tanks, pipelines, and buildings. News films showed people sunk to their hips in the liquefied ground, requiring assistance to extricate themselves.*

Several large apartment buildings, though structurally sound, slowly settled and tilted in the liquefied soil, one at an angle of 85 degrees to the vertical. The movement took place slowly and no one was hurt, but the experience was intensely frightening. In other places, fountains of water and sand spouted up from the ground, leaving holes surrounded by low craters of sand.

Liquefaction was also responsible for much of the damage to buildings in the waterfront area of San Francisco during the 1906 earthquake. However, the reason for the extensive damage was not recognized until many years later, because liquefaction was not understood in 1906. In later earthquakes in California, two earth dams were victims of liquefaction within the dams themselves. The Sheffield Dam collapsed during the 1925 Santa Barbara earthquake, flooding a large region of the city, and the Van Norman Dam was damaged beyond repair in the 1971 San Fernando earthquake, necessitating the evacuation of tens of thousands of people from their homes. Both of these dams were constructed of hydraulically filled earth, a type of construction that is no longer used. Even the small landslides along the shore of Lake Merced in San Francisco (in the 1957 Daly City earthquake, magnitude 5.3) were the result of liquefaction.

As a general rule, liquefaction is most likely to occur in low-lying areas near the seacoast or adjacent to bays, marshlands, rivers, and lakes. Sand layers often exist in such places, and the soil is usually soft and saturated with water. Examples in California are the landfill areas around San Francisco Bay, ocean-beach developments along the Pacific Coast, and much of the Los Angeles basin. Maps showing the potential for liquefaction in various regions of California are available and should be consulted if you plan to build in such areas.

To remedy the problems of liquefaction is not simple, so people often decide to take their chances. The most obvious remedy is to avoid building on any site where the potential for liquefaction is high. However, if a builder is determined to proceed, three methods are available for reducing the likelihood of liquefaction. The first method, called vibroflotation, is a process for compacting the sand so that it is less likely to liquefy. A heavy device that can be vibrated is placed in the ground, and water is forced into the ground at the same time. The combination of vibration and added water causes the sand to liquefy, after which it is compacted by the heavy device. New sand is added to fill up the extra space. When the work is finished, a firm, dense layer that is resistant to liquefaction has replaced the potentially liquefiable sand layer. The second method consists of using

* There is no danger of being completely submerged in liquefied soil, or even in quicksand, because the soil is much heavier per unit of volume than the human body.

Liquefaction of the underlying soil caused these apartment buildings in Niigata, Japan, to slowly tilt and settle after the June 1964 earthquake (magnitude 7.5). The buildings were so well designed structurally that no cracks appeared in the walls. No one was hurt. One woman was on the roof of the center building hanging up her wash when the earthquake struck; when the roof reached the ground, several minutes later, she jumped safely off. (Courtesy of George Housner, California Institute of Technology, and NOAA/EDIS)

underground drains to remove the water in the sand layer; once the soil is drained, conditions for liquefaction no longer exist. The third method is simply to excavate and remove the layer that is subject to liquefaction. Because all three of these methods are expensive, they are not very attractive to owners and builders.

Ground Subsidence

Another serious and all-too-common hazard from earthquakes is subsidence of the land surface. During earthquake ground shaking, compaction of the soil particles occurs because the individual soil grains are rearranged to take up less space—watch what happens to the contents of a box of breakfast cereal when it is vibrated. When the total volume of soil is reduced in this manner, the land settles, forming a depression. The settlement results in tilting of the land and the formation of cracks and fissures, causing damage to buildings, roads, bridges, and pipelines. No amount of careful design will save these facilities when the ground on which they rest becomes terra non firma.

Soils that are easily compressed are the most likely to create subsidence problems during earthquakes. Filled lands, especially in formerly swampy areas, are in this category. When building on such soils, the owner has no simple remedies available. An obvious plan is to remove the offending material, but since this may be extremely expensive, it is more common to build a foundation that goes through the poor material into a firmer layer below. Pile foundations are usually used for this purpose, but these, too, are very expensive.

During the 1906 earthquake, considerable subsidence occurred in San Francisco in regions where the land had been filled in, particularly along the waterfront and in swampy areas farther inland. In places the subsidence was more than a meter, resulting in badly cracked streets and buildings as well as broken underground pipes. The 1976 Tangshan earthquake in China also brought about extensive settlement of the ground, especially along the seacoast near Bohai Bay. Irrigation systems were badly damaged, and a coastal village that settled 3 meters was permanently flooded by the sea.

Earthquakes and Dams

The collapse of a dam as the result of an earthquake is a frightening possibility, especially to those millions of people who live in potential flood zones below dams. Movie makers are well aware of the opportunities for creating exciting scenes based upon this hazard, and so earthquakes in the movies usually involve a dam that is trembling and cracking and on the verge of letting go.

The region vulnerable to flooding by the collapse of a dam extends far below the site of the dam itself, so that people often are unaware that they live or work in an area of potential flooding. For example, in the immediate vicinity of San Francisco Bay there are 226 dams; over half a million people live on the flood plains of those dams. Lower Crystal Springs Reservoir could flood large areas of the city of San Mateo; Lexington Reservoir could do the same to San Jose; Calaveras Reservoir to Fremont; Lake Chabot to San Leandro; and San Pablo Reservoir to San Pablo. Similar hazards exist in Sacramento, Los Angeles, San Diego, and other major cities. Of course, dams are inspected regularly for their seismic safety, and if they are judged to be unsafe, the owners are required to lower the water levels.

During the 1971 San Fernando earthquake (magnitude 6.6) both the Upper and Lower Van Norman Reservoir dams were strongly shaken for about 15 seconds. These dams are located north of the San Fernando Valley, directly above a heavily populated area; both are of earth-fill construction. The shaking was strong enough to induce liquefaction of the soil within the dams themselves. The dams lost their strength and suffered great damage. The Upper Dam moved about 2 meters downstream, its crest settling about 1 meter. In spite of these large movements, the dam

Lower Van Norman Dam nearly collapsed in the 1971 San Fernando earthquake. Much of the top of the dam slid into the reservoir. People living below the dam were evacuated while the water level was lowered by draining and pumping. (Photo by R. E. Wallace, courtesy of USGS)

held the water behind it. The danger of collapse was imminent, however, especially from large aftershocks, so the reservoir was drained as rapidly as possible.

The Lower Dam, about a kilometer downstream, met a similar fate; a large portion of the upstream side of the dam slid into the reservoir. If the water level had been a meter higher, or if the shaking had lasted a few seconds longer, the dam would surely have collapsed and released the water. As it was, no one could be sure that the dam would continue to hold, so about 80,000 people living in the flood zone of the dam had to be evacuated. It took four days for the water in the reservoir to be drawn down to a safe level, after which people were allowed to return to their homes. Since that time a new reservoir, called Los Angeles Reservoir, has been built midway between the two damaged ones and has effectively replaced them. The repaired upper reservoir is now operated with very limited storage, and the lower one serves as a flood control basin with no permanent storage.

Although we have focused attention on the disastrous behavior of the two Van Norman dams, we should also point out that many other dams came through the San Fernando earthquake unscathed. Within 40 kilometers of the epicenter were 28 other dams, varying in height from 10 to 60 meters. None of these dams suffered significant damage. A notable performance was that of Pacoima Dam, a concrete arch dam located almost directly over the earthquake source. Extremely large ground accelerations (over $1.0g$, where g is the acceleration of gravity) were recorded at the left abutment of this dam, and the canyon below the dam was subjected to numerous small landslides, yet the dam itself suffered no damage. The explanation is simple enough—this and most of the other dams were built recently, and the designers gave adequate consideration to seismic effects. In contrast, the Lower Van Norman Dam was built in 1915, before liquefaction and the effects of seismic shaking were well understood.

Hebgen Lake Dam in Montana, just west of Yellowstone National Park, was subjected to very strong ground shaking during the earthquake (magnitude 7.1) of August 17, 1959. This dam is on the Madison River, just upstream from Earthquake Lake, which was formed by the landslide previously described. The dam is constructed of earth-fill and has a core wall of concrete that extends vertically through both the dam and the underlying foundation soil. During the earthquake the crest of the dam dropped about 2 meters and cracks appeared both in the earth fill and in the concrete core. Waves in the reservoir, caused by the large vertical earth movements, overtopped the dam several times. Nevertheless, the dam held back the water and no flooding occurred.

The failure of Sheffield Dam during the 1925 Santa Barbara earthquake (magnitude 6.3), as we have noted, was also caused by liquefaction. The epicenter of the earthquake was about 17 kilometers away. The dam was of earth-fill construction and was located above the eastern part of the city. A portion of the dam slid downstream about 30 meters, releasing 150 million liters (40 million gallons) of water to flood a large area. Today there is a new dam, with the same name.

Adobe Construction

Throughout many parts of the world, people live in houses that are constructed of inexpensive building blocks. We generally refer to this kind of construction as "adobe construction," although it takes many forms and uses a great variety of materials other than true adobe. All buildings of this type have certain common features—thick walls of unreinforced blocks or bricks of poor material, weak cement or mortar, heavy roofs, and no ties to hold together the walls and roofs. They are built by unskilled labor of inexpensive, readily available, natural building materials. The techniques of construction have been handed down for generations in each region where it exists. Adobe is the accepted form of construction in rural villages in Central and South America, northern Africa, parts of the Middle East and Asia, China, and the Philippines. Unfortunately, these regions of the world are highly seismic, and adobe construction is deadly during earthquakes.

The hazards of adobe construction were all too evident in the 1976 Guatemala earthquake, which occurred at 3:00 A.M., when most people were in their homes. Most of the 23,000 deaths were caused by the collapse of adobe houses in the small rural villages located along the line of the Motagua fault. Over 300 villages suffered severe damage; in some villages, practically every building collapsed.

In Guatemala, adobe structures consist of heavy adobe bricks held together by mud mortar. The roofs are of thatch, tile, or corrugated metal, supported

Adobe buildings are highly susceptible to severe earthquake damage. This Guatemalan rural village was almost totally destroyed in the 1976 earthquake. Dozens of other communities along the Motagua fault suffered the same fate. (Photo by Robert W. Madden, courtesy of National Geographic Society)

by horizontal beams resting on adobe walls. When the walls collapsed, the roofs came down too, and the inhabitants had little chance for survival. This form of construction is all that is available to many people, and so rebuilding of homes in the same traditional way began immediately after the earthquake. In this respect, the Guatemala experience parallels that of other countries that have suffered earthquake disasters.

The need to develop simple, inexpensive methods of construction to replace adobe has long been recognized, but it is not an easy matter to change building customs that have been followed for generations. Programs of mass education and practical instruction in new building techniques are required.

Table 3-1
Principal Earthquake Hazards

Natural Hazards
Ground shaking
Ground failures (cracks and offsets)
Landslides, avalanches, mud flows
Liquefaction
Subsidence
Tsunamis
Seiches

Man-made Hazards
Damage to (or collapse of) buildings, bridges, and other structures
Floods from dam failures and water pipeline breaks
Fires from tank failures and gas pipeline breaks
Falling and overturning of objects inside and outside of buildings
Disruption of transportation, communication, power, water supply, and sewer systems
Radioactive leaks from nuclear reactors

At Ofunato, on the Sanriku coast of Japan, a tsunami that began on the continental shelf off the coast of Chile tossed this fishing boat on top of a house. The tsunami took 22 hours to make the 11,500 mile journey at an average speed of 500 miles per hour. The earthquake (magnitude 8.5) occurred on May 22, 1960. (Photo by A. Shimbun, courtesy of K. Ishida)

4

Tsunamis

Huge waves approached at a speed much faster than we expected.... I saw children carried away by the waves to their deaths.
—Eyewitness report of the May 1983 tsunami
off the coast of Japan

CHENEGA ISLAND IS USUALLY a quiet and peaceful place. Situated a few miles off the coast of Alaska in the southwestern part of Prince William Sound, it was the home of 80 people before March 27, 1964. Many of the residents lived by hunting and fishing, and life on Chenega was strenuous but simple. Besides the houses, there was a church, a schoolhouse, a cemetery, and a pier for fishing boats.

Good Friday in 1964 was a "pretty day" according to one resident, with the sea relatively calm and children playing on the beaches. Then the great earthquake came. The earth trembled violently, and some of the islanders, knowing that a sea wave might follow, looked toward the shoreline. Nicholas Kompkoff spotted his three daughters down by the pier, just as he also noticed the waters receding from the beach. He ran quickly to the girls, snatching the two youngest in his arms. The third, aged 10, scrambled beside him up the hill. Even as they were running, a huge wave arrived "before the ground even stopped shaking," as Mary Kompkoff related. Sweeping 30 meters (100 feet) up the hillside, it carried away people, the church, and every single home. Only the schoolhouse and the cemetery remained. All else was swept away. Two of the Kompkoffs' daughters, including the eldest, were carried off by the wave, gone forever. Nicholas and the other child were tossed farther up the hill and knocked unconscious, but miraculously they survived. All told, 23 of the 80 inhabitants of Chenega Island were killed by the giant wave.

Wreckage in Crescent City, California, from the 1964 tsunami that originated in Alaska, 1,600 miles away. Eleven people who returned to the waterfront area too soon after the evacuation were killed by subsequent tsunami waves. (Photo courtesy of U.S. Army Corps of Engineers)

The survivors spent the cold night huddled around bonfires on high ground above their ruined village; the next day they were evacuated by boat and airplane across the sound to Cordova. Two fishing boats from Chenega, unharmed because their owners were out fishing in them, were used in the evacuation. The people eventually moved to new homes elsewhere. Nicholas and Mary Kompkoff moved to Anchorage, but they, like the other survivors, made plans to reestablish their village someday, and in 1983, a group of them returned to an island not far from Chenega.

From Alaska to Crescent City

On that same Good Friday in 1964, the people of Crescent City, California, more than 2,500 kilometers (1,600 miles) from Chenega Island, were warned that a seismic sea wave, or tsunami, had been generated off the coast of Alaska. What effect it would have as it traveled across the Pacific Ocean no one knew with any certainty. As a precaution, people were evacuated from waterfront areas in Crescent City and other places along the North American coast. About four hours after the great wave struck Chenega Island, a wave arrived at Crescent City. The time was about 20 minutes before midnight. That first wave rose to a height of only

1 meter in the harbor and did no damage, so some of those who had been evacuated earlier from the waterfront area returned, thinking that the danger had passed. For a few, this action was fatal, because during the next two hours several more waves arrived. The largest, 6 meters high, came about an hour and a half after the first wave.

During its nighttime rampage in Crescent City harbor, the tsunami destroyed several hundred buildings and killed 11 people. A 25-ton concrete tetrapod that was part of the harbor breakwater was carried onto the land. The waves overturned cars and carried logs and debris into the streets. Houses were moved, a pier was twisted, and 23 boats anchored in the harbor were sunk or capsized. Fifty-four homes were destroyed and many others damaged. Fires started when five oil storage tanks were ruptured. Rescue and cleanup work began immediately, but rebuilding and repair took many months. To avoid another catastrophe in the future, the city was rezoned to locate businesses on higher ground, and a public park was built in the low-lying waterfront area.

Disasters similar to those at Chenega Island and Crescent City take place every few years somewhere around the edges of the Pacific Ocean. In May of 1983 a strong earthquake under the Sea of Japan, off the west coast of the main Japanese island of Honshu, created a tsunami that killed 105 people, including a group of school children who had just arrived for a picnic on the beach near the city of Akita. The coastal harbors of Japan, especially those along the northeast coast of Honshu Island, known as the Sanriku coast, are frequently the targets of damaging tsunamis. Most Japanese tsunamis originate with earthquakes in the nearby Japan and Ryukyu trenches, but occasionally they travel from much more distant places such as Alaska and South America. Destructive tsunamis have also been experienced along the western coast of North America, the Aleutian Islands, the Philippines, New Guinea, Indonesia, the islands of the South Pacific, Hawaii, Peru, Chile, and Central America. Much less common, but equally destructive, have been tsunamis in the Caribbean Sea, eastern Atlantic Ocean, Mediterranean Sea, and Indian Ocean.

The Japanese word "tsunami" is now used throughout the world to describe an ocean wave created by an earthquake. Its literal meaning is bay or harbor wave; the name originated from the fact that tsunamis appear as large surface waves only when inside a bay or harbor (tsunamis are virtually undetectible in the open ocean). Another name for a tsunami is "seismic sea wave," which is both descriptive and accurate. However, the term "tidal wave," often used in newspaper reports, is obviously incorrect because tsunamis are not related to the tides, which are caused by the moon and the sun. To avoid confusion, the term tidal wave should be reserved for waves (such as the famous ones in the Bay of Fundy) that are created by true tides.

Causes of Tsunamis

Most large tsunamis are created by sudden vertical movements of the seafloor during earthquakes. Such movements occur in subduction zones where one crustal plate (usually an oceanic plate) is moving downward into the earth beneath an adjacent plate. The world map (Figure 2-1, p. 14) shows the major subduction zones around the Pacific Ocean. The triangular symbols on the plate boundaries show the directions of movement of the subducting, or descending, plates. For instance, along the Aleutian Islands the Pacific plate is being pushed downward beneath the plate to the north (which is actually part of the North American plate), and off the coast of South America the Nazca plate is descending under the South American plate. When a plate descends, it creates a deep ocean trench and a range of volcanic mountains (on a continent) or a row of volcanic islands (in the sea). Of special interest to people living in northern California, Oregon, Washington, and British Columbia is the San Juan de Fuca plate, a small plate being pushed eastward and subducting under the North American plate. It is presumed to be responsible for the volcanic activity of the Cascade Range, including Mount St. Helens.

As the stresses build up between the descending and the overlying plates, relief occurs in the form of sudden slippage, which, of course, is an earthquake. Since the slippage involves upward movement of the sea bottom, it also causes an upward movement of the overlying sea water. When a large volume of sea water is suddenly uplifted, huge surface waves are created that spread outward in all directions. When these waves rush onto the land at a nearby coast, as they did at Chenega Island, they are called *local tsunamis*. These local waves have caused great loss of life on the coasts of Japan, the Philippines, South America, and the eastern Mediterranean Sea.

The sudden uplift of the seafloor also creates a series of underwater waves that travel great distances across the oceans. These waves are not like ordinary waves that we see on the surface; rather, they are like sound waves or shock waves that travel *through* the water. The wave front extends from the surface of the ocean all the way to the bottom. Such a tsunami moves at very high speed, often 600 to 800 kilometers per hour (400 to 500 miles per hour). It was one of these *distant tsunamis* that created havoc at Crescent City. When a tsunami reaches a coastline, its energy is concentrated in a smaller and smaller wave front, because the ocean depth decreases. The tsunami then creates surface waves that rush up onto the coast, like huge breakers, or, in a narrow harbor, the tsunami may create a *bore* of water. A bore is an onrushing flood of water with a high, abrupt front; when a bore strikes the shore, its effects are similar to that of a large breaker. Observers in Hilo, Hawaii, reported that a bore entering the harbor in 1960 (from the Chile tsunami) sounded like a freight train approaching.

Detailed investigations undertaken after the 1964 Alaska earthquake clarified the mechanism by which a tsunami is generated. Changes in land elevations at hundreds of locations in the zone of uplift could be observed and measured—primarily because the uplift occurred in a region of many islands (Figure 4-1), each of which provided a bench mark. The mechanism is illustrated in the cross section (Figure 4-2), which shows the Pacific plate being driven beneath the continental plate. This movement

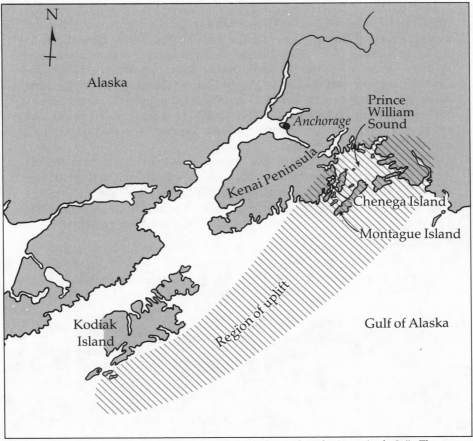

Figure 4-1. Region of uplift during the great 1964 Alaska earthquake (magnitude 8.4). The ocean floor was uplifted in a zone about 500 miles long and 60 miles wide. At Montague Island the land was raised over 30 feet. The tsunami traveled outward from the zone of uplift in all directions, but the principal direction was perpendicular to the long axis of the uplifted zone (that is, southeast, toward Crescent City and the coasts of Oregon and northern California).

causes pressures against the continental plate in the northward direction (arrow A) as well as downward (arrow B). Hence, the top surface of the continental plate tends to be deformed downward near the region of contact between the plates. When the 1964 earthquake occurred, the two plates slipped along their contact zone, allowing the continental plate to jump upward. The abrupt upward movement of the seafloor was the cause of the tsunami. The region of the seafloor that moved upward was about 800 kilometers (500 miles) long and about 100 kilometers (60 miles) wide. The maximum upward displacement was over 10 meters on Montague Island.

The local tsunamis created by this uplift caused much damage along nearby coasts, as at Chenega Island. However, the main tsunami that spread out across the Pacific Ocean caused damage primarily along the western coast of North America. The waves were highly directional in character because of the elongated shape of the uplifted region. The shape was such as to "aim" the tsunami toward the coasts of Canada and the United States, which explains why major tsunami damage occurred there while Japan and Hawaii suffered no significant damage. In contrast, earthquakes occurring farther west in the Aleutian Islands usually create tsunamis that travel directly toward Hawaii and Japan and have little effect on the North American coast.

Only in recent decades have we learned how tsunamis are generated, yet Charles Darwin came remarkably close to understanding their causes when he felt the devastating earthquake of February 20, 1835, at Concepción, Chile, during the voyage of the *Beagle*. Here is how he described the resulting tsunami, based upon reports he gathered from eyewitnesses:

> Shortly after the shock, a great wave was seen from the distance of three or four miles, approaching in the middle of the bay with a smooth outline; but along the shore it tore up cottages and trees, as it swept onwards with irresistible force. At the head of the bay

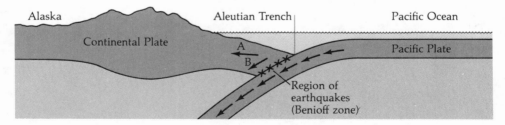

Figure 4-2. Cross section of plates in southern Alaska. The Pacific plate is being subducted under the continental plate, creating earthquakes along the zone of contact (Benioff zone). The descending Pacific plate pushes the continental plate northward (arrow A) and downward (arrow B). When the 1964 Alaska earthquake occurred, strain was released and the continental plate rebounded upward, raising the seafloor and generating the tsunami.

The tsunami created by the 1964 Alaska earthquake was so powerful that it carried fishing boats into the center of Kodiak, Alaska. (Photo by U.S. Navy, courtesy of USGS)

it broke in a fearful line of white breakers, which rushed up to a height of 23 vertical feet above the highest spring-tides. Their force must have been prodigious; for at the Fort a cannon with its carriage, estimated at four tons in weight, was moved 15 feet inwards. A schooner was left in the midst of the ruins, 200 yards from the beach. The first wave was followed by two others, which in their retreat carried off a vast wreck of floating objects. In one part of the bay, a ship was pitched high and dry on shore, was carried off, again driven on shore, and again carried off.

He then goes on to describe the movements of the sea and changes in land elevations:

The most remarkable effect of this earthquake was the permanent elevations of the land; it would probably be more correct to speak of it as the cause. There can be no doubt that the land around the Bay of Concepción was upraised two or three feet. . . . On the Island of Santa Maria the elevation was greater; on one part, Captain FitzRoy found beds of putrid mussel shells still adhering to the rocks, ten feet above high-water mark.

Thus, Darwin was aware that along the coast of Chile earthquakes were

Facts about Tsunamis

Most tsunamis are caused by earthquakes that occur under the oceans, especially around the edges of the Pacific Ocean. Potential danger areas are along the coast and in harbors and bays at low elevations—say, less than 15 meters above sea level for tsunamis of distant origin and less than 30 meters above sea level for tsunamis of local origin.

- A tsunami is not a single wave, but a series of several waves. Therefore, stay out of danger areas (harbors, bays, estuaries, and along the coast) until all of the waves have passed, which may take several hours.
- The size of a tsunami cannot be predicted. It may generate a small wave in one place and a giant wave somewhere else. Every tsunami is potentially dangerous.
- Pay attention to tsunami warnings for distant earthquakes. In 1960, 61 people were killed and several hundred injured in Hilo, Hawaii, although warnings had been issued for 10 hours before the arrival of the first wave.
- Any earthquake occurring off the coast may generate a local tsunami. If you feel such an earthquake, immediately move away from the shoreline. In May 1983, over 100 people were killed in Japan by a tsunami that struck the northwestern coast of Honshu, although everyone in the vicinity felt the earthquake and should have heeded it as a warning.
- The approach of a tsunami may be heralded by a noticeable rise or fall of the water level along the shoreline. This signal should always be taken as a warning.
- Never go down to the beach to watch for a tsunami. When you see the wave coming, it is probably too late to escape.

accompanied by uplifting of the land, and accordingly he expressed his ideas on the causes of mountain building: "It is hardly possible to doubt that this great elevation has been affected by successive small uprisings, such as that which accompanied or caused the earthquake of this year."*

Tectonic displacements of the seafloor are not the only geologic phenomena that cause tsunamis. Just as dramatic are volcanic eruptions, such as that of Krakatoa on August 27, 1883. This volcanic island, located in the Sunda Strait between Java and Sumatra, erupted in such a huge explosion that the ash it projected into the atmosphere completely encircled

* Darwin, Charles, *The Voyage of the Beagle.*

the earth, and red sunsets persisted for months. The great tsunami it generated was observed at seaports throughout the world and destroyed a total of 5,000 ships. Together, the eruption and the tsunami accounted for 36,000 deaths. An even more violent eruption was that of the volcanic

The tsunami from the 1964 earthquake in Alaska had sufficient force to drive this plank through a truck tire in Whittier, Alaska. (Photo courtesy of USGS)

island of Santorin (or Thera) in the Aegean Sea; archeologists have dated the eruption at approximately 1450 B.C. It created a tsunami that did great damage along shorelines throughout the eastern Mediterranean region. Underwater landslides also may cause tsunamis, but such slides are not very common, and usually their effects are small and localized.

How Tsunamis Travel

The way in which tsunamis travel is quite different from that of the ordinary surface waves we see on the ocean. As already mentioned, they do not travel on the surface but, like sound waves, they travel through the body of the ocean with the wave front extending from the surface to the seafloor.

The speed of a tsunami is surprisingly high; for instance, tsunamis in the Pacific Ocean usually travel at 600 to 800 kilometers per hour, although even higher speeds have been observed. The speed in the open ocean depends primarily upon the depth of the water, although other features may also have an effect. In deep water the speed (s) is approximately equal to the square root of the acceleration of gravity (g) times the depth of the ocean (d), as expressed by the formula

$$s = \sqrt{gd}$$

This equation shows that the deeper the water, the higher the speed. Even though it travels fast, a tsunami still takes many hours to cross the Pacific Ocean (some typical travel times are listed in Table 4-1). Thus, while there may be little warning for people living near the source of a tsunami, there should be ample warning for those living at great distances.

Another remarkable feature of a tsunami is its long period. The period of a wave is the time interval between the arrival of two successive waves. Most of us are familiar with the periods of ordinary surface waves on the ocean; if you stand on a beach and watch the waves roll in, you discover that the periods are usually in the range of 5 to 15 seconds. But tsunamis have periods that range from five minutes to an hour. It is difficult to visualize a wave having such a long period that the second wave reaches the shore an hour after the first one, but that is not uncommon with tsunamis.

Table 4-1
Tsunami Travel Times in the Pacific Ocean

Alaska to California, 4 to 7 hours	*Note:* The time depends upon the location of the earthquake source, the nature of the generating mechanism, and the place where the tsunami arrival is observed. Typical speeds are 600 to 800 kilometers per hour (400 to 500 miles per hour).
Alaska to Hawaii, 4 to 6 hours	
Alaska to Japan, 4 to 8 hours	
Chile to Hawaii, 14 to 15 hours	
Chile to Japan, 22 to 23 hours	
Japan to Hawaii, 7 to 8 hours	

The wave period seems to depend upon where the tsunami originates. The tsunami that accompanied the 1964 Alaska earthquake was generated by the sudden uplifting of a large part of the shallow continental shelf, and it had a main wave with a period of 1.7 hours. This extremely long period may be related to the natural period of vibration (or resonant period) of the relatively wide and shallow body of water on the continental shelf. In contrast, the 1946 and 1957 Aleutian earthquakes occurred in the narrow and deep Aleutian trenches, and their tsunamis had periods from 7 to 15 minutes.

Even though a tsunami travels within the body of the ocean, it may still create a small surface wave. (We are referring now to the travel of the tsunami in the open ocean, not at the shoreline.) The height of the wave is typically less than 50 centimeters (20 inches), which is less than the height of ordinary wind-generated surface waves. This means that the tsunami is imperceptible to people on boats or ships. Nor can it be seen from the air. The unfortunate result is that the existence of a tsunami cannot be verified until the wave reaches shore. During the 1946 tsunami in Hilo, the crew of a freighter standing about a kilometer offshore were amazed to see huge waves breaking over the tops of buildings on shore, yet they themselves never felt the wave as it went past their ship.

Even if the ocean were perfectly calm and you were sitting in a canoe in the middle of the ocean, you probably would not detect a tsunami. The reason is that the wave is extremely flat, being very long and low. As an example, the wave might be 200 kilometers long and 50 centimeters high;

Taken from the deck of the *Brigham Victory*, April 1, 1946, this photograph shows a tsunami destroying a pier inside Hilo harbor. (Courtesy of NOAA/EDIS)

Residents flee before an onrushing tsunami in Hilo, Hawaii, on April 1, 1946. The wave can be seen breaking through the tall palm trees in the background. The earthquake took place five hours earlier in the Aleutian Islands. (Courtesy of Joint Tsunami Research Effort)

such a wave might take 15 minutes to pass by, and you would not even be aware of it.

Tsunamis completely change their characteristics when they approach the coast or enter a harbor. The tsunami is transformed into a surface wave that increases in height as it approaches the shore; it then becomes a breaker that crashes onto the land and runs up for a considerable distance. It is this wave that has inspired the misleading term "tidal wave." Breakers as high as 10 meters were reported inside Hilo harbor from the 1960 tsunami. However, the height of a wave or bore cannot be predicted because it depends upon such complicated factors as the orientation of the bay, the focusing effect of the harbor, the topography of the sea bottom, and resonance effects within the bay or harbor (Hilo harbor has a well-defined resonant period of 18 minutes).

The number of successive waves in a tsunami is also unpredictable. Sometimes only one large wave appears in a harbor, while other times there is a series of several waves (as at Crescent City in 1964). Because the waves are separated by such long periods, people are liable to assume prematurely that the tsunami danger is over. To be on the safe side, you should allow at least an hour for the arrival of the next wave (for a distant tsunami). If none comes, then it is probably safe to return to the affected area.

Sometimes the first visible sign of a tsunami is a lowering of the water level at the shoreline. Stories are told of people walking onto exposed tidelands to pick up flopping fish, only to be drowned by an incoming tsunami. Actually, there is no uniformity in tsunami behavior; sometimes the initial effect is a lowering of the water level, but just as often the tsunami begins with the water rising.

Hilo Harbor

The city of Hilo, second largest in the Hawaiian Islands, is particularly vulnerable to tsunamis because it is located in the path of waves emanating from both the Aleutian and the Peru-Chile subduction zones. In addition, the topography in and around the harbor is ideal for causing large amplification of the surface waves. The harbor is V-shaped, with the narrow part toward the downtown part of the city, and the sea bottom rises smoothly toward the shore; thus, the harbor creates a funneling effect both horizontally and vertically.

Not surprisingly, Hilo has been severely damaged by tsunamis on two occasions in recent decades. On April 1, 1946, a tsunami originated in the Aleutians and swept into Hilo harbor five hours later, having traveled 3,800 kilometers (2,400 miles) at 780 kilometers per hour (480 miles per hour). The waves rushed into the waterfront area, destroying buildings, piers, ships, and cars. Even the Hilo breakwater was torn apart over much of its length. The death toll was 96 in Hilo alone, 173 in all of Hawaii. In an attempt to prevent future disasters, the city created a buffer zone along the harbor by building a narrow park and roadway. Unfortunately, the zone was too small and rebuilding was permitted within parts of the tsunami-damaged area. Fourteen years later, another tsunami struck with similar results.

This time, on May 22, 1960, the tsunami originated in Chile and arrived at Hilo early the next morning, about 15 hours after the earthquake. The tsunami traveled 10,500 kilometers (6,500 miles) at an average speed of 700 kilometers per hour (430 miles per hour). The largest wave rose to a height of 12 meters (40 feet), poured over a seawall 3 meters high, and entered the downtown area. Part of the city was totally demolished, 61 people were killed, and scores of others were injured. Here is an eye-witness account of the third wave:

> At first there was only the sound, a dull rumble like a distant train, that came from the darkness far out toward the mouth of the bay. By 1:02 A.M. all could hear the loudening roar as it came closer through the night. As our eyes searched for the source of the ominous noise, a pale wall of tumbling water, the broken crest of the third wave, was caught in the dim light thrown across the water by the lights of Hilo. . . . At 1:04 A.M. the 20-foot high, nearly vertical front of the inrushing bore churned past our look-

out, and we ran a few hundred feet toward safer ground. Turning around, we saw a flood of water pouring up the estuary. . . . Dull grating sounds from buildings ground together by the waves and sharp reports from snapped-off power poles emerged from the flooded city now left in darkness behind the destroying wave front. . . . By 2:15 A.M. the height of the waves reaching the bay front had diminished sufficiently that it appeared to be safe to enter Hilo to assess the damage. Thick slimy mud covered the streets, and fish abandoned by the water that carried them over the seawall were strewn about. Hilo's sewage, dumped inside the harbor entrance, had been stirred up by the first two waves and hurled into the face of the city by the third, filling the air with a distressing stench. . . . Stores in the block north of Haili Street had been breached by the waves, which gathered up their contents and dumped them in confusion on the streets. . . . The row of stores that had walled the west side of Kamehameha Avenue was gone. . . . Large boulders and smashed cars littered the streets. . . . Across from the Cow Palace four people had emerged from the window of a second-story apartment in one of the few buildings that remained along the street. The lower floor had been gutted and the stairs carried away. With poles salvaged from the debris that cluttered the streets, we helped the numbed survivors to the ground.*

After this second disaster, rebuilding in the zone of flooding was not permitted. Instead, a park was built along the waterfront, beautifying the city and providing a safety zone between the shoreline and the built-up areas.

A Local Tsunami in Hawaii

Inhabitants of the geologically active "Big Island" of Hawaii are familiar with volcanic eruptions, lava flows, and earthquakes, especially along the southeastern coast on the slopes of Kilauea. On November 29, 1975, at 3:36 A.M. local time, a magnitude 5.7 earthquake awakened people in this region, including 32 people camped on the beach at Halape, about 30 kilometers west of Kalapana. A few campers got up and moved away, but most went back to sleep. At 4:48 A.M. a magnitude 7.2 earthquake, the main shock, occurred. The campers reported they were unable to stand during the strong shaking. Within a minute they saw the sea rise and become a wave washing onto the land. Then a second, larger wave washed trees, rocks, and people into a deep crack (5 to 7 meters deep) in which

---

* Eaton, J.P., Richter, D. H., and Ault, W. U., "The Tsunami of May 23, 1960, on the Island of Hawaii," *Bulletin of the Seismological Society of America*, vol. 51, no. 2, April 1961, pp. 135-157.

The business district on Kamehameha Avenue in Hilo, Hawaii, was wrecked by the 1946 tsunami. (Magoon Private Collection, courtesy of NOAA/EDIS)

they were churned uncontrollably, as if "inside a washing machine," according to one survivor. One person died by being drowned or battered to death, another was swept out to sea and presumed dead, and 19 others were injured. The wave traveled about 100 meters inland with a maximum run-up height of 12 meters. The land itself moved toward the sea about 6 meters and subsided about 3.5 meters, so that a former coconut palm grove is now standing in the sea.

The damage was not confined to the Halape camping area, however. In nearby communities houses were destroyed, piers damaged, and automobiles tumbled about. Many aftershocks followed during the next two weeks, and the earthquake triggered a small volcanic eruption from Kilauea.

How to Reduce Tsunami Damage

Damage from tsunamis is the result of waves and bores moving through harbors and breaking onto the land. The damage is usually of the following kinds:

- Flooding due to the rapidly rising water level
- Dynamic loading on structures when struck by moving water, especially bores
- Debris impact, that is, debris carried by the moving water is smashed into structures and other objects
- Erosion around foundations from the rapidly moving water
- Damage to moored ships from waves, changes in water level, and battering against piers

Breakwaters constructed to stop ordinary surface waves also offer some protection against tsunamis; however, large tsunamis can sweep around and even over them. San Francisco Bay is protected from tsunamis by its narrow opening.

To prevent damage to structures and facilities, the best plan obviously is to build in locations away from tsunami-prone areas. When this is not feasible, structures can be designed to withstand some of the tsunami effects. For instance, a building can be positioned with its long direction parallel to the path of the waves, thus offering its smallest area to be struck and also providing the greatest strength (in the long direction of the building) to resist the impact forces. It also is desirable to make the first floor of the building as "open" as possible, using only light walls between the main columns. Then the tsunami can sweep through the first floor, tearing out the light walls and moving furniture but doing minimum damage to the structure itself. This concept is used in the Hawaiian Islands for beachfront hotels as well as homes. You can see homes constructed on tall poles with the ground level completely open (for use as a carport) and with the first floor about 3 meters above the ground.

Tsunami Warning Systems

Monitoring systems for detecting earthquakes are now so well developed throughout the world that seismologists are immediately aware of any earthquake that occurs in a location where tsunamis are known to have been generated in the past. Whether or not a tsunami has indeed been generated will not be known until it strikes a shoreline, either near the source or at some distant place. For this reason, anyone who is located in a coastal area, especially in Alaska, Japan, and western South America, should immediately move away from the shoreline when an earthquake is felt. However, when tsunamis are moving across the Pacific Ocean, there will be many hours of notice.

The idea of an official tsunami warning system for the Pacific Ocean was conceived by personnel of the U.S. Coast and Geodetic Survey after the 1946 tsunami that damaged Hawaii so severely. Intended at first only for Hawaii, it was later expanded into a warning system for the entire Pacific Ocean. Today the Pacific Tsunami Warning System (PTWS) is based at the Honolulu Observatory and is operated by the National Oceanographic and Atmospheric Administration (NOAA), which took over the U.S. Coast and Geodetic Survey in 1970. Seismograph and tide gauge stations have been set up on islands around the edges of the Pacific; these stations report directly to the Honolulu station. In addition, a new type of pressure gauge has recently been developed for detecting tsunamis in the open ocean, and these may prove useful in detecting tsunamis before they reach the shore.

When an earthquake occurs anywhere around the Pacific Ocean, the warning system is alerted. If the earthquake is of sufficient magnitude and located where it could cause a tsunami, a "tsunami watch" is issued. This is a message to all stations that the possibility of a tsunami exists. From the known travel times of tsunamis, each station estimates the time of arrival of the potential tsunami. Stations nearest the earthquake will be on the lookout for the arrival of waves. When information is received that a tsunami actually exists, a "tsunami warning" is sent out to the entire area that might be affected by the tsunami, along with its estimated time of arrival. The progress of the tsunami is monitored, and the warnings are updated and repeated as new information is received. Inhabitants of coastal regions are warned by local government officials, and sometimes evacuations are ordered.

The Crescent City, California, disaster in 1964 affords a good illustration of how the warning system works. (It also illustrates how little the general population knows about tsunamis.) The Good Friday earthquake took place in Alaska at 5:36 P.M. (local time) on March 27, 1964, and was recorded at seismograph stations around the world. The possibility of a tsunami was immediately recognized and advisory messages were sent out from the Honolulu station. At 7:55 P.M. the Kodiak, Alaska, station reported that a seismic sea wave was experienced at 6:35 P.M., with water levels 3 to 4 meters above mean sea level. The existence of a tsunami having been confirmed, Honolulu issued a warning that a tsunami "was spreading over the Pacific Ocean." Expected arrival time at Oahu was 11:00 P.M., approximately five and a half hours after the earthquake. At 9:08 P.M. the Kodiak station reported that a 10-meter wave had occurred at 6:40 P.M. and a 12-meter wave at 8:30 P.M.

In Crescent City, people in low-lying areas were warned by the police, and evacuations were carried out. The first wave arrived at Crescent City at 11:39 P.M. (local time in California, which is two hours ahead of Alaska time), about four hours after the earthquake. A second wave arrived at 12:30 A.M., another at 12:45 A.M., and the largest at 1:40 A.M. After the first two waves, which caused only minor flooding, some people returned to the area to clean up; the third and fourth waves engulfed several of them and caused most of the damage. In Hawaii and Japan the damage was relatively minor due to the directional aspects of the tsunami. The tsunami reached Japan about 7 hours after the earthquake, Kwajalein in 10 hours, and Peru in 15.5 hours. After the tsunami had passed, Honolulu sent out its final bulletin advising that the danger was over.

Table 4-2
Some Famous Tsunamis

Date	Origin	Remarks
c.1450 B.C.	Island of Santorin (or Thera) in the Aegean Sea; volcanic eruption	Violent explosion of Santorin volcano destroyed the island. Huge tsunami affected coasts of the eastern Mediterranean region, bringing death and destruction.
A.D. 365 July 21	Eastern Mediterranean region; large earthquake (50,000 deaths)	Tsunami drowned 5,000 people in Alexandria.
1755 Nov. 1	Lisbon, Portugal (off the coast, in the Atlantic Ocean); earthquake of magnitude 8.6 (60,000 deaths)	Several large waves washed ashore in Portugal, Spain, and Morocco. Major damage and many deaths in Lisbon from tsunamis.
1835 Feb. 20	Chile (off the coast, near Concepción); earthquake of magnitude 8.5	Damaging tsunami described by Charles Darwin, who felt the earthquake during the voyage of the *Beagle*.
1868 Apr.2	Island of Hawaii (south slope of Mauna Loa); volcanic earthquake of magnitude 7.7	Local tsunami destroyed many houses and killed 46 people.
1868 Aug. 13	Chile and Peru (along the coast near Arica); earthquake of magnitude 8.5 (25,000 deaths)	Several large waves devastated Arica (now in Chile but then in Peru). Damage in Hawaii.
1883 Aug. 27	Island of Krakatoa (in the Sunda Strait, between Java and Sumatra); volcanic eruption (36,000 deaths)	Violent explosion of Krakatoa volcano. Great tsunami felt in harbors around the world. Tsunami caused much damage and loss of life on nearby islands.
1896 June 15	Japan (off the Sanriku coast); earthquake of magnitude 7.5 (27,000 deaths)	Numerous villages entirely destroyed by tsunami; maximum wave height 15 meters. Many lives lost by drowning.
1918 Oct. 11	Puerto Rico (off the western coast, under the Mona Passage); earthquake of magnitude 7.5 (116 deaths)	Tsunami caused damage and 40 deaths.
1923 Sept. 1	Japan (Tokyo and vicinity); earthquake of magnitude 8.3 (99,300 deaths)	Known as the Kanto earthquake (epicenter in Kanto Plain). Major damage over a large area, including Tokyo and Yokohama; great fire in Tokyo. Tsunami in Sagami Bay struck the shore 5 minutes after the earthquake; maximum wave height 10 meters. Tsunami killed 160 people.
1933 Mar. 3	Japan (off the Sanriku coast); earthquake of magnitude 8.9 (3,000 deaths)	Major damage and most deaths from tsunami; maximum wave height 24 meters.
1944 Dec. 7	Japan (off the southern coast of Wakayama Prefecture); earthquake of magnitude 8.3 (1,000 deaths)	Known as Tonankai earthquake. Large tsunami along coast from Shikoku Island to Shizuoka.

Date	Origin	Remarks
1945 Nov. 28	Pakistan (off the coast); earthquake of magnitude 8.3 (4,100 deaths)	Tsunami struck the coast.
1946 Apr. 1	Aleutian Islands (south of Unimak Island in the Aleutian trench); earthquake of magnitude 7.5 (173 deaths)	Major damage in Hilo, Hawaii (96 deaths). Minor damage in California (one death in Santa Cruz).
1946 Dec. 21	Japan (off the southeast coast of Shikoku Island); earthquake of magnitude 8.4 (1,360 deaths)	Known as the Nankai earthquake. Great tsunami caused much damage and loss of life along south coast of Shikoku Island and Kii Peninsula.
1952 Mar. 4	Japan (off the southeastern coast of Hokkaido); earthquake of magnitude 8.3 (31 deaths)	Known as the Tokachi-Oki earthquake. Tsunami struck the coasts.
1956 July 9	Greece (Dodecanese Islands); earthquake of magnitude 7.8 (53 deaths)	Tsunami struck the coasts.
1960 May 22	Chile; Arauco Province (along the continental shelf, near the coast, south of Concepción); earthquake of magnitude 8.5 (2,230 deaths)	Major damage in Hilo (61 deaths), and Japan (120 deaths). Wave height 5 meters on Sanriku coast of Japan. Local tsunami in Chile.
1964 Mar. 27	Gulf of Alaska; earthquake of magnitude 8.4 (131 deaths)	Known as the Good Friday earthquake. Major tsunami damage to seaports and coastlines in Alaska; numerous deaths, including 23 at Chenega Island. Damage to ports in British Columbia, Washington, Oregon, and California (notably Crescent City, where 11 people were killed).
1964 June 16	Japan (Niigata); earthquake of magnitude 7.5 (26 deaths)	Large tsunami caused coastal flooding.
1968 May 16	Japan (off the coast; east of Hachinohe); earthquake of magnitude 8.6 (48 deaths)	Also known as the Tokachi-Oki earthquake. Tsunami damage to many buildings and port facilities in Hachinohe and Hakodate.
1975 Nov. 29	Island of Hawaii (southeastern coast); earthquake of magnitude 7.2	Local tsunami. Severe damage in vicinity of Kalapana and Hanape; 2 deaths, both from tsunami.
1976 Aug. 17	Philippine Islands (Moro Gulf); earthquake of magnitude 8.0 (6,500 deaths)	Major damage and many deaths from tsunami.
1977 Aug. 19	Indonesia (south of Sumbawa Island); earthquake of magnitude 8.0 (189 deaths)	Tsunami destroyed several villages.
1979 Dec. 12	Colombia (off the coast); earthquake of magnitude 7.9 (600 deaths)	Tsunami caused much damage and loss of life.
1983 May 25	Japan (west of Honshu Island in the Japan Sea); earthquake of magnitude 7.7 (106 deaths)	Tsunami struck the coast near Akita and caused 105 deaths.

The first known earthquake-detecting device. The famous Chinese scholar Chang Heng constructed it in Xian in 132 during the Han dynasty. In a large vessel, six feet in diameter, he placed a pendulum that could move in eight directions. Eight corresponding dragons, each with a ball in its mouth, were mounted on the outside of the vessel. When earthquake movement caused the pendulum to swing, the ball was knocked out of the dragon's mouth and caught in the open mouth of a toad below. At the same time, a noise was emitted by the instrument, notifying observers that an earthquake had occurred. By noting which toad held the ball, they could tell the direction from which the earthquake came. Chang Heng's instrument worked so well that it recorded distant earthquakes not felt by the observers themselves. The original device has long since disappeared, but visitors to Xian can see this small-scale replica.

5

How Earthquakes and Their Effects Are Measured

I ran out of my cabin, both glad and frightened, shouting, "A noble earthquake! A noble earthquake!" feeling sure I was going to learn something.

—John Muir, *The Yosemite*

DESCRIBING AN EARTHQUAKE by saying, "It had a magnitude of 6.2" is analogous to describing a person by saying, "He weighs 165 pounds." Is he tall or short, young or old, pleasant or mean? You know none of these characteristics from his weight, although you probably would bet on him in a boxing match with an opponent who weighs 140 pounds.

So it is with the well-known Richter scale of earthquake magnitude— it gives you only a single measurement of a very complex phenomenon. As we will see later, this measurement is the maximum amplitude, or height, of the seismic waves generated by the earthquake as measured under certain standard conditions. But the earthquake has many other important features: How long did the strong shaking last? How large an area of the fault was fractured? How far below the ground surface did the earthquake occur? From the magnitude number alone, we know little about what happened during the earthquake—just as from his weight, we know nothing of a person's character, personality, or appearance. Nevertheless, the magnitude scale provides a useful means of comparing earthquakes by size.

Several magnitude scales are in use by seismologists, but because Richter magnitude is the best known, we will explain how it is obtained and what

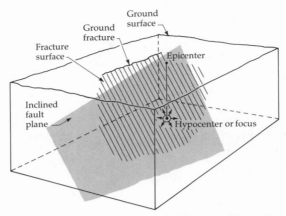

Figure 5-1. Fracture surface. An earthquake is the fracturing of the rocks along a fault plane. If the fracture reaches the ground surface, a visible ground fracture line is created. The hypocenter is the point on the fracture surface where the earthquake begins; the epicenter is at the ground surface, directly over the hypocenter.

it means. To do so, we must provide some background information about earthquake mechanisms, seismic waves, and recording instruments.

Earthquake Mechanisms

As we explained in Chapter 2, an earthquake is produced when the rocks making up the earth's crust are fractured due to the buildup of excessive strains, usually the result of plate movement. The fracture takes place over an irregular area lying along a more-or-less plane fault surface (Figure 5-1) that may be vertical or inclined. The length of the fault break may be from a few meters in a nearly imperceptible earthquake to a few hundred kilometers in a great earthquake. Furthermore, the fracture surface may reach the ground level or may remain far below. In general, the longer the length of fault that fractures, the greater the magnitude of the earthquake.

As with any tearing or breaking action, the earthquake begins at a specific point and then spreads outward. The point where the fracture begins is the *hypocenter* or *focus* of the earthquake, and the point on the surface of the earth directly above the hypocenter is the *epicenter*. Thus, a map showing the locations of earthquakes is actually a map of epicenters. The distance from the ground surface to the hypocenter, called the *hypocentral depth* or *focal depth*, may be from a few kilometers to several hundred kilometers. Shallow-focus earthquakes, such as those along the San Andreas fault, typically have depths between 5 and 40 kilometers. Along the western coast of South America, as well as in other subduction zones, deep-focus earthquakes occur along the Benioff zone at depths up to 500 kilometers, or 300 miles (see Figure 2-2, p. 17).

A fault scarp created by the 1980 El Asnam, Algeria, earthquake.

The relative displacement, or *offset*, between the rocks on opposite sides of the fault surface is also highly variable. In small earthquakes the offset may be only a few centimeters, but in the 1906 San Francisco earthquake it was 6 meters (near the epicenter, which was located in Marin County, north of San Francisco). During the 1971 San Fernando, California, earthquake, the vertical offset between opposite sides of the fault was about 1 meter, and a vertical *scarp* of that height was formed. The 1954 Fairview Peak, Nevada, earthquake created a scarp 3 meters high, and the El Asnam, Algeria, earthquake of 1980 created one 4 meters high.

After the earthquake fracture begins, it spreads rapidly along the fault surface, releasing the strain energy that was stored in the rocks (just as the strain energy of a stretched rubber band is released when the band breaks). Of course, a measurable amount of time is required for the fracture to occur (think of tearing a sheet of paper from one end to the other). In a small earthquake the fracturing will be over in a few seconds, but in a great earthquake it lasts for many seconds. As an example, in the 1906 San Francisco earthquake it took more than a minute for the San Andreas fault to rupture from the hypocenter in Marin County southward through the San Francisco peninsula to some point south of San Juan Bautista, a

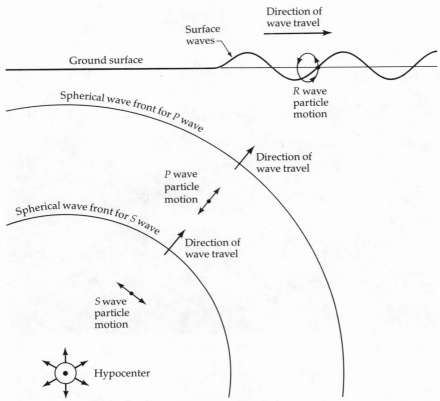

Figure 5-2. Seismic waves. The *P* and *S* waves are body waves that radiate outward in all directions from the places where fractures are occurring. The first motion you feel during an earthquake is usually the *P* wave. Surface waves travel along the surface, somewhat like water waves, and typically arrive after the *P* and *S* waves.

distance of over 200 kilometers. At the same time, the fault was also rupturing northward from the hypocenter. From this example, we see that the source of an earthquake is not only the focal point, but the moving fracture lines, which explains why a large earthquake lasts much longer than a small one.

As the fracturing process takes place, *energy* is released from the rocks at the leading edges of the fracture. Most of the released strain energy is dissipated by breaking and crushing the rocks, moving the adjoining blocks of the earth both vertically and horizontally, and creating heat. A small part of the energy is radiated outward in all directions in the form of *seismic waves*, which travel through the body of the earth. When the waves reach the earth's surface they create the motion of the ground that we feel during an earthquake. Since the waves originate at the moving fracture lines and not at a single point, and since they bend and reflect as they travel within the earth, they reach us at various times and from more than one direction. The result is that the recorded patterns of seismic waves are a composite of many individual waves.

Seismic Waves

"First there was a sudden jolt that made me lose my balance for a second. Then I could feel the ground moving, and a second, stronger jolt came. After a few seconds of shaking, a rolling and swaying motion started, like being on a boat. The swaying lasted until the earthquake ended. There was noise all the time."

Here we have an actual description of the sensations experienced during a moderate earthquake. The ground motion felt by the observer was caused by the various kinds of waves arriving at his location. Seismic waves are of two principal types—*body waves* that travel within the body of the earth, somewhat like sound waves, and *surface waves* that travel along the ground surface, like waves on the ocean. The two jolts were from the arrivals of two different types of body waves, and the subsequent rolling motion was caused by the surface waves.

The body waves are generated directly by the fracturing rocks. They radiate outward in every direction, diminishing in intensity as they move farther from the source (Figure 5-2). Several types of body waves are created by reflection and refraction when the seismic waves encounter different materials within the earth and when they reach the surface. However, the two principal types of body waves are the P (or primary) and S (or secondary) waves. The P waves, traveling faster than the S waves, are the first to arrive at a given location and are responsible for the initial jolt, signaling that an earthquake has occurred. The S wave usually follows in a few seconds, causing another, typically sharper jolt.

Although the body waves travel continuously away from the source along a spherical wave front, the individual particles of material within the earth move in an alternating manner, ending up approximately where they started. In the case of P waves, the particles of matter move forward and backward along a line in the same direction as the wave travels, hence the P wave is sometimes called a "push-pull" wave. As the particles move back and forth, they alternately compress and stretch the material, in the same manner as an underwater sound wave. This movement can be visualized by considering the coil spring shown in Figure 5-3. When the end of the spring is moved suddenly to the right, a wave travels to the right along the full length of the spring, although the individual coils move back and forth and return to their initial positions. At any given instant, portions of the spring are compressed, while other parts are stretched.

The S waves are quite different, because the individual particles oscillate

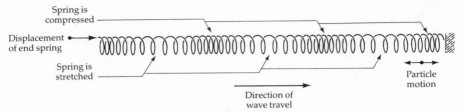

Figure 5-3. Motion of the ground during passage of P waves is analogous to that of a coil in a spring when one end of the spring is displaced. A wave travels along the spring from one end to the other, alternately compressing and stretching the coils. Individual coils move only back and forth.

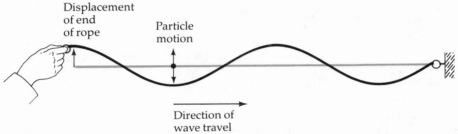

Figure 5-4. Motion of the ground during passage of S waves is represented by moving one end of a rope up and down. Although the wave travels the length of the rope, individual particles of the rope move only up and down, perpendicular to the direction of wave travel.

along a line perpendicular to the direction of wave travel; for this reason, the S waves are sometimes called transverse waves. (Since S waves produce shear stresses in the material instead of compression, they are also known as shear waves.) Their action can be visualized by moving the end of a rope up and down (Figure 5-4). A wave will travel to the right along the rope, although individual particles of the rope move only up and down, perpendicular to the line of the rope.

Because all parts of the earth, whether solid rock in the crust or molten rock in the core, can transmit compression, the P waves can travel throughout the entire body of the earth. However, the molten parts of the earth's interior cannot transmit shear stresses, hence the S waves are restricted to the solid crust.

Surface waves travel over the land surface, penetrating only a short distance below ground level. Some of the damaging ground motion in earthquakes comes from these waves, which travel at a slower speed and have longer periods (or lower frequencies) than do the body waves. Surface waves are also of several types; the two most important are the R (or

Raleigh) waves and the *L* (or Love) waves, named for the British scientists, Lord Raleigh and A.E.H. Love, who first identified them. The *R* waves behave like water waves, which move continuously forward although the individual particles move in an elliptical path in a vertical plane (Figure 5-2). This type of motion can be observed when a cork or twig floats on a pond; if a stone is tossed into the water, the resulting waves cause the object to move up and down, as well as back and forth, as the waves pass by, but the object always returns to its initial position. The *L* waves also travel continuously forward, but the individual particles move back and forth in a horizontal plane, in a direction perpendicular to the direction of wave travel.

At any given point on the surface of the ground, the motion we feel is the result of several kinds of waves. The measurement of this ground motion is a difficult task, yet it is from such measurements that the magnitudes and other characteristics of earthquakes must be determined.

Seismographs

The motion of the ground is recorded during earthquakes by instruments known as *seismographs*. These instruments were first developed around 1890, so we have recordings of earthquakes only since that time. Today, there are hundreds of seismographs installed in the ground throughout the world, operating as part of a worldwide seismographic network for monitoring earthquakes and studying the physics of the earth. The records produced by seismographs, called *seismograms*, are used in calculating the location and magnitude of an earthquake.

A typical seismogram is shown in Figure 5-5. The horizontal axis indicates time (measured in seconds) and the vertical axis gives the ground displacement (usually measured in millimeters). Thus, the seismogram shows how the ground moves with the passage of time. When there is no earthquake, the seismogram will be a straight line except for the presence of small wiggles caused by local disturbances or "noise." To record earthquakes that may be thousands of kilometers away, the instrument must greatly amplify the ground motion, typically between 5,000 and 80,000 times.

The seismogram is actually obtained from a moving internal part of the seismograph known as a *seismometer*, which may be a pendulum or a mass mounted on a spring. The seismometer also contains a damping mechanism that is essential for an accurate recording of the ground motion. The movement of the seismometer is converted into a seismogram by any of several means—a pen drawing an ink line on paper revolving on a drum, a light beam making a trace on a moving photographic film, or an electromagnetic system generating a current that is recorded electronically on tape.

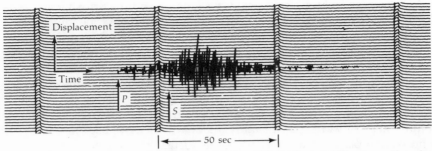

Figure 5-5. Seismogram of an aftershock of the May 1983 Coalinga, California, earthquake (recorded at the Terman Engineering Center, Stanford University). The arrivals of the *P* and *S* waves are indicated by arrows (21 seconds apart). The distance from the seismograph to the epicenter was 130 miles.

The motion of the ground at any point is three-dimensional, which means that the point moves in space and not merely in a plane or in a straight line. To completely record this motion, three seismometers must be built into each seismograph. These seismometers move in three perpendicular directions, two horizontal and one vertical, and generate three corresponding seismograms. Each seismogram is labeled according to its direction—compass direction if it records horizontal motion and "up-down" if it records vertical motion. Knowing how the ground moved in three perpendicular directions, seismologists can calculate the actual movement in space.

Locating Earthquakes

Because they travel at different speeds and come from various sources, the *P*, *S*, *R*, and *L* waves arrive at the recording station at different times. Skilled interpreters are able to examine the seismograms and identify the initial arrivals of the various waves. The exact time of arrival of each wave can be determined from the time scale.

From the arrival times of the *P* and *S* waves, seismologists can calculate the distance from the instrument to the hypocenter of the earthquake (Figure 5-6), provided that the speed of travel of each wave is known. Information on speeds of seismic waves has been accumulated for many years, so today the speeds are known with good accuracy. The speeds are different for *P* and *S* waves, and they vary depending upon the material through which the waves are traveling. In bedrock, typical speeds are 3 to 8 kilometers per second (7,000 to 18,000 miles per hour) for *P* waves and 2 to 5 kilometers per second (4,500 to 11,000 miles per hour) for *S* waves. Once the distance from each recording station to the hypocenter has been calculated, the hypocenter and the epicenter can be located. Only then can the Richter magnitude be calculated.

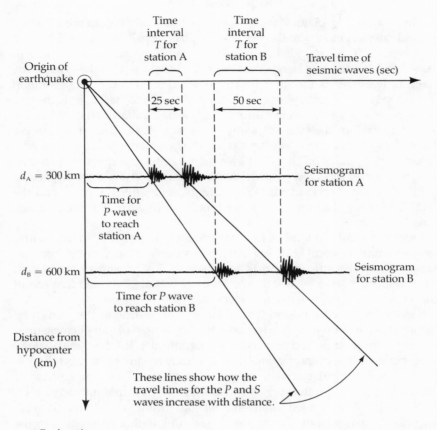

Explanation:

The *P* waves travel faster than the *S* waves, hence they reach the seismograph first. Let *T* represent the time interval (measured on the seismogram) between the arrival of the *P* and *S* waves at a given seismographic station. Also, let *P* and *S* represent the travel speeds of these waves. Then the distance *d* from the station to the hypocenter is calculated from the following formula:

$$d = T \left(\frac{PS}{P - S} \right)$$

Example:

$P = 6 \, \text{km/sec} \quad S = 4 \, \text{km/sec}$

Station A: $\quad T = 25 \, \text{sec} \quad d_A = (25 \, \text{sec}) \left(\frac{6 \times 4}{6 - 4} \, \text{km/sec} \right) = 300 \, \text{km}$

Station B: $\quad T = 50 \, \text{sec} \quad d_B = (50 \, \text{sec}) \left(\frac{6 \times 4}{6 - 4} \, \text{km/sec} \right) = 600 \, \text{km}$

The earthquake hypocenter is 300 km from station A and 600 km from station B.

Figure 5-6. How the distance to the hypocenter is determined.

Richter Magnitude

The magnitude of an earthquake is actually a measurement of the ground displacement (or the particle displacement) as obtained from a seismogram. The ground displacement is the same as the amplitude of the seismic waves, and hence the larger the wave motion, the greater the magnitude of the earthquake. Many people contributed to the evolution of the magnitude concept, but it remained for Dr. Charles F. Richter, a professor at the California Institute of Technology in Pasadena, to actually set up a scale on the basis of many years of observations and to apply the scale to well-known earthquakes. He explained the scale in a now classic paper published in 1935.* Professor Richter is a quiet and modest man who never attached his own name to the scale. He even refused to call it the Richter scale in his later writings, long after the press and the public had made "Richter scale" synonymous with "earthquake magnitude scale."

Professor Richter often has trouble explaining to people that the Richter scale is a mathematical scale involving measurements and calculations on paper. "They seem to think it is some sort of instrument or apparatus. Every year they come by wanting to look at my scale," he said in a recent interview with a newspaper reporter.

Richter borrowed the term "magnitude" from astronomy, in which he had an amateur interest. In astronomy the brightness of stars is measured on a logarithmic scale and referred to as magnitude. But there the analogy ends, because in astronomy smaller magnitude means greater brightness (Sirius, the brightest star outside the solar system, has a magnitude of 1.0, and the faintest stars visible to the eye have a magnitude of 6.0). Furthermore, Richter used a conventional logarithmic scale to the base 10, whereas the astronomers' scale uses logarithms with a base equal to the fifth root of 100 (approximately 2.51).

Because the amplitudes of the seismic waves diminish with distance from the hypocenter, it is necessary to agree on a standard distance at which the amplitude will be measured. Richter set this distance as 100 kilometers (62 miles) from the epicenter. (Since he was dealing only with shallow earthquakes, the epicentral and hypocentral distances were almost the same.) Of course, no instrument is likely to be located just 100 kilometers from the epicenter, so corrections are made to convert the measurements obtained at other distances to what they would have been at 100 kilometers. These corrections are not precise, which is one reason for the differences in Richter magnitude reported for the same earthquake by different seismographic stations.

* Richter, C. F., "An Instrumental Earthquake Magnitude Scale," *Bulletin of the Seismological Society of America*, vol. 25, no. 1, January 1935, pp. 1-32.

Another difficulty arises because there are many kinds of seismographs in use, and they record different maximum wave amplitudes even when they are located at the same place. Richter worked with a particular instrument known as the Wood-Anderson short-period torsion seismograph, and if another instrument is used (which is generally the case now), a correction is required to arrive at the amplitude that would have been obtained with the standard instrument. The variability in these corrections is another reason why there are discrepancies in the calculations of magnitudes.

Finally, the quantity to be measured and the units of measurement must be decided upon. For Richter magnitude, the maximum amplitude of the ground displacement, as recorded on the seismogram, is measured in microns; a micron (or micrometer) is one-millionth of a meter. The Richter magnitude is the logarithm (to the base 10) of this amplitude.

The definition of magnitude is stated best in Richter's own words: "The magnitude of any shock is taken as the logarithm of the maximum trace amplitude, expressed in microns, with which the standard short-period torsion seismometer would register that shock at an epicentral distance of 100 kilometers." It is simple enough to measure the wave amplitude on a seismogram; all of the difficulties in determining magnitude arise when converting this measurement to what it would have been if measured on the Wood-Anderson seismograph at a distance of 100 kilometers from the epicenter. Each seismographic station has complicated correction formulas that it uses for this purpose; these formulas take into account distance and direction to the epicenter, focal depth, and local geologic conditions. To make possible rapid determination of magnitude, the formulas are programmed on computers or plotted as charts. Then, when an earthquake occurs, and after its epicentral distance has been determined, the observer merely measures the maximum amplitude on the seismogram and goes to the chart or computer program to obtain the magnitude.

This procedure is illustrated in a simplified way in Figure 5-7, which is constructed for a particular seismographic station. Because the correction factors are different for each location, different charts are required for other stations. Assume that a particular earthquake generated a seismogram with a maximum amplitude of 20 millimeters, measured directly from the seismogram in the manner shown at the top of the chart. Also, assume that the seismograph was located 300 kilometers from the epicenter. These two points are located on the left- and right-hand scales and connected by a straight line. Where the line crosses the middle scale, we read the Richter magnitude, which is 5.3.

The Richter magnitude scale is both empirical and imprecise. As Richter remarked about the magnitude in his original paper, "Precision in this matter was neither required nor expected. What was looked for was a method of segregating large, moderate, and small shocks, which should be

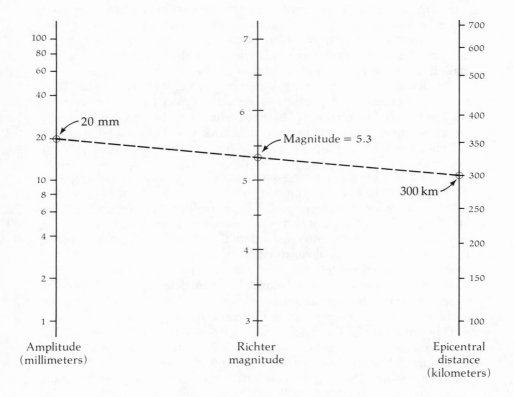

To determine Richter magnitude, you first must obtain the epicentral distance to the earthquake (e.g., 300 km). Then proceed as follows:
(1) Measure the amplitude on the seismogram (e.g., 20 mm)
(2) Draw a straight line connecting the amplitude and the epicentral distance
(3) Read the Richter magnitude on the central scale (e.g., 5.3)

(Note: This chart is for a particular seismographic station; each station uses a different chart.)

Figure 5-7. Chart for determining Richter magnitude.

based directly on instrumental indications, and thus might be freed from the uncertainties of personal estimates or the accidental circumstances of reported effects. . . . Lest the impression should be created that great precision is being claimed for this method, it is desirable here to emphasize its actual crudity."

In current practice, magnitude determinations from different stations vary by several tenths of a unit; in other words, for a particular earthquake, one station may assign a magnitude of 6.3, another 6.8, and another 6.5. This amount of variability is to be expected when one considers the great complexity of the earthquake process and the fact that the seismic waves may travel through many different types of rocks and crustal formations between the hypocenter and the seismograph.

Interpreting Richter Magnitude

Because the scale is logarithmic, each step in magnitude means a tenfold increase in amplitude of wave motion, or ground displacement. An earthquake of magnitude 6.0 has ten times as great a wave amplitude as does an earthquake of magnitude 5.0, a hundred times the wave amplitude of a magnitude 4.0 earthquake, and one thousand times the wave amplitude of a magnitude 3.0 earthquake. A magnitude of 0 (zero) does not mean no earthquake; since zero is the logarithm of 1, such an earthquake has an amplitude of 1 micron (or one thousandth of a millimeter) on the standard seismograph at 100 kilometers. A magnitude 0 earthquake is indeed small, imperceptible to humans, but quite capable of being recorded on sensitive instruments. Even smaller earthquakes can be detected and measured; an earthquake of magnitude -1 has an amplitude of 0.1 microns under the standard conditions, and so on for magnitudes of -2, -3, etc. The limit of detectability is about magnitude -3 for the most sensitive of seismographs. The smallest earthquakes felt (no matter how slightly) by humans are about magnitude 1.5, and the smallest earthquakes causing damage (albeit very minor damage) are about magnitude 4.5.

The scale itself imposes no upper limit to magnitude, because it is a calculated quantity. For this reason, the Richter magnitude scale is often said to be an "open-ended" scale. In reality, the earth itself provides a practical upper limit, just as the sensitivity of the measuring instruments provides a lower limit. The largest earthquakes ever recorded had magnitudes of 8.9; there have been two such earthquakes since recordings began, both in subduction zones under the sea. One took place off the coast of Japan in 1933 and the other off the coast of Ecuador in 1906. It is likely that the earth is not capable, in a physical sense, of creating earthquakes larger than those. The table of earthquake data (see Table A-1,

Even wood houses fell down in the 1923 Kanto earthquake (magnitude 8.3) that killed 99,300 people. The severe shaking was followed by a fire that swept through Tokyo and a tsunami that devastated harbor facilities around Tokyo Bay. (Courtesy of K. Ishida)

p. 173), gives the rate of occurrence of large earthquakes throughout the world.

Seismic Energy

Richter magnitude is closely related to the energy released in an earthquake. As explained previously, only a few percent of the released energy is radiated in the form of seismic waves. But since these waves are responsible for the ground motion that we feel and for the resulting damage to buildings and structures, we shall refer to this radiated energy as the *seismic energy* of the earthquake. Although it constitutes but a small part of the total, the seismic energy of an earthquake of magnitude 8.0 would supply a day's total electrical energy consumption for the entire United States.

Many investigations have been made by seismologists attempting to determine the amount of seismic energy released in earthquakes of various magnitudes. At best, any such determination is empirical and quite approximate. Dr. Beno Gutenberg, late Caltech seismologist and colleague of Richter, arrived at the following equation relating energy to Richter magnitude:

$$\text{Log } E = 9.9 + 1.9M - 0.024M^2$$

In this equation, the left-hand side is the logarithm to the base 10 of the seismic energy E expressed in ergs, and M is the Richter magnitude. As we will explain shortly, this equation shows that the amount of seismic energy increases at a tremendous rate as the magnitude increases. But, to be systematic, we first ought to explain what an erg is. An erg is a common unit of energy in the old metric system, just as the foot-pound is a unit of energy in the U.S. system. The conversion between them is as follows:

$$1 \text{ foot-pound} = 13.6 \times 10^6 \text{ ergs}$$

In the modern metric system, known as SI (Système International d'Unités), the unit of energy is the joule, which is 10^7 ergs. Another unit of energy in SI is the kilowatt-hour, a unit used in the United States by the utilities when they sell electrical energy to household customers:

$$1 \text{ kilowatt-hour} = 3.6 \times 10^6 \text{ joules} = 3.6 \times 10^{13} \text{ ergs}$$

To give further meaning to the erg, we note that the daily electrical energy consumption in a typical U.S. household might be 15 kilowatt-hours, or 5.4×10^{14} ergs. Also, the total electrical energy consumption in the United States is about 300×10^{21} ergs per day.

Now let us relate the erg to seismic energy, in accord with Gutenberg's equation. With calculator in hand, we set M equal to 4, run through the equation, and obtain $E = 0.0013 \times 10^{20}$ ergs. This value is tabulated in the first line of Table 5-1. Doing the same thing with $M = 5, 6, 7,$ and 8, we get the remaining values. The first thing that strikes us is the rapid rate of increase of seismic energy with increase in magnitude. For instance, a magnitude 5.0 earthquake releases 48 times as much energy as does a magnitude 4.0 earthquake. Continuing to examine the numbers in the table, we see that an earthquake of magnitude 8.0 releases 35 times as much energy as does one of magnitude 7.0, and one of magnitude 7.0

Table 5-1
Seismic Energy of Earthquakes

Richter Magnitude	Seismic Energy (ergs)	Energy Ratio for Each Unit Increase in Magnitude	Energy Ratio Compared to a Magnitude 4.0 Earthquake
4.0	0.0013×10^{20}		1
5.0	0.063×10^{20}	48	48
6.0	2.7×10^{20}	43	2,100
7.0	110×10^{20}	39	80,500
8.0	$3,700 \times 10^{20}$	35	2,800,000

releases 39 times as much energy as does one of magnitude 6.0. Thus, a magnitude 8.0 earthquake releases about 1,300 times as much energy as does a magnitude 6.0 earthquake. Proceeding in this manner, we see that it would take about 2,800,000 earthquakes of magnitude 4.0 to release as much seismic energy as a single magnitude 8.0 earthquake. This realization shows the fallacy of thinking that many small earthquakes will forestall the occurrence of a great earthquake. While the smaller earthquakes do indeed release energy, the amount is relatively unimportant when compared to the energy released in a great earthquake.

Yet another way to make energy comparisons is shown in Figure 5-8. The vertical axis represents energy in ergs and the horizontal axis represents Richter magnitude. The energy scale is logarithmic, so that each step on the scale represents a tenfold increase in energy. The sloping line gives the relationship between energy and magnitude as obtained from Gutenberg's equation. Again we observe the tremendous increase in energy with increase in magnitude. Since the seismic energy we are considering is the radiated energy, it is probably more representative of the destructive capacity of an earthquake than is the magnitude itself. This means that a magnitude 8.0 earthquake is 35 times more threatening (not 10 times) than is a magnitude 7.0 earthquake.

Because of the inherent difficulties in obtaining a meaningful magnitude number by measuring the wave amplitude on a seismogram, seismologists are turning to a new quantity, known as *seismic moment*, as a better physical measure of earthquake size. Seismic moment is more difficult to explain and to calculate than is magnitude, and at present it is used primarily in research. We have not yet seen it reported in newspaper accounts of earthquakes.

Accelerographs

Seismographs are designed to record small ground displacements caused by distant earthquakes and are used by seismologists interested in locating hypocenters, estimating magnitudes, and studying the mechanics of earthquakes. On the other hand, engineers are interested in what happens to structures subjected to strong ground shaking from nearby earthquakes—the kind of shaking that causes damage. To record this type of ground shaking requires a different type of instrument, one that measures ground acceleration instead of ground displacement. Such instruments are called *accelerographs*, and the mass-spring system within the accelerograph is called an *accelerometer*. The record generated, known as an *accelerogram*, has the general appearance of a seismogram, but its mathematical characteristics are quite different. Accelerographs do not have a continuous recording system, as seismographs do; instead, they are triggered by an earthquake and operate from batteries (because the

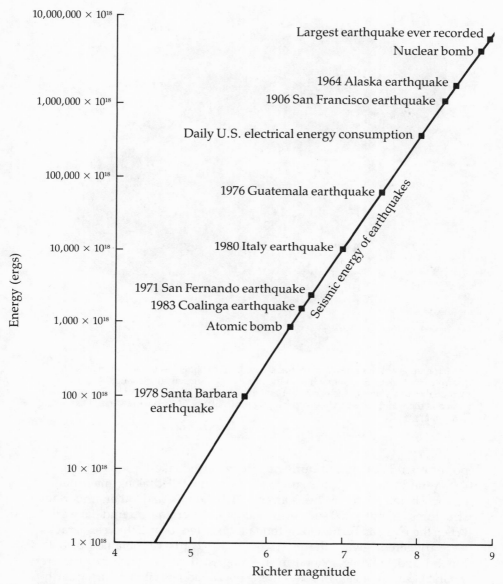

Figure 5-8. Seismic energy versus Richter magnitude. The energy scale is logarithmic; the amount of energy is multiplied by 10 for each step on the vertical scale. Thus, the 1980 Italy earthquake (magnitude 7.0) had approximately 100 times the energy of the 1978 Santa Barbara earthquake (magnitude 5.7).

Accelerographs are designed to measure strong local earthquakes but are insensitive to distant earthquakes. Seismographs, on the other hand, are sensitive enough to detect earthquakes anywhere in the earth, but go off scale when an earthquake occurs nearby. Shown is the widely used SMA-1 accelerograph. (Courtesy of Kinemetrics Inc., Pasadena, California)

power often is disrupted during a strong earthquake).

Several hundred accelerographs are now installed along major faults in the United States as well as in tall buildings and other important structures. About 5,000 such instruments are operating around the world. When the 1971 San Fernando earthquake occurred, over 250 accelerographs were triggered, giving the most complete records yet obtained of both ground and building motion in a strong earthquake. Such records are invaluable to engineers in determining how buildings vibrate during earthquakes.

Intensity

Centuries ago, people tried to rate the size of an earthquake according to the amount of damage it caused. If one earthquake shook down more buildings than another, it was assumed to be the larger of the two. While

John Muir and His Bucket of Water

The great naturalist John Muir was sleeping in his little wood cabin below Sentinel Rock in Yosemite Valley when, on March 26, 1872, he felt the great Owens Valley earthquake. For years before, Muir had speculated about the origins of the many spectacular talus slopes along the bases of the huge granite walls. Now he was to have a personal demonstration of at least one of the causes.

To quote Muir: "At half-past two o'clock of a moonlit morning in March, I was awakened by a tremendous earthquake, and though I had never before enjoyed a storm of this sort, the strange thrilling motion could not be mistaken, and I ran out of my cabin, both glad and frightened, shouting, 'A noble earthquake! A noble earthquake!' feeling sure I was going to learn something."

The ground shook so violently that Muir had to walk carefully, balancing himself "as if on the deck of a ship among waves." He feared that parts of the rock cliffs above him would be shaken down, so he took shelter behind a large yellow pine. As he looked up toward the cliffs in the moonlight, he saw Eagle Rock (on the south wall of the valley) give way, sending thousands of boulders falling toward the valley floor. After first inspecting the new talus slope, Muir ran across the meadow to the Merced River to see which way it was flowing; he "was glad to find that *down* the valley was still *down*." A second shake startled him at about 3:30 A.M., and a third came still later. He said the earthquakes came nearly every day for over two months.

Muir kept a bucket of water on his table to observe the sloshing and to learn what he could about the shaking. In studying earthquakes today, we have much more than a bucket of water; but we still have to wait for earthquakes to happen in order to "learn something."

(Courtesy of the Bettman Archive)

Table 5 - 2
Modified Mercalli (MM) Intensity Scale

I Not felt by people.[1]

II Felt only by a few persons at rest, especially on upper floors of buildings.

III Felt indoors by many people. Feels like the vibration of a light truck passing by. Hanging objects swing. May not be recognized as an earthquake.[2]

IV Felt indoors by most people and outdoors by a few. Feels like the vibration of a heavy truck passing by. Hanging objects swing noticeably. Standing automobiles rock. Windows, dishes, and doors rattle; glasses and crockery clink. Some wood walls and frames creak.

V Felt by most people indoors and outdoors; sleepers awaken. Liquids disturbed, with some spillage. Small objects displaced or upset; some dishes and glassware broken. Doors swing; pendulum clocks may stop. Trees and poles may shake.

VI Felt by everyone. Many people are frightened, some run outdoors. People move unsteadily. Dishes, glassware, and some windows break. Small objects fall off shelves; pictures fall off walls. Furniture may move. Weak plaster and masonry D cracks.[3] Church and school bells ring. Trees and bushes shake visibly.

VII People are frightened; it is difficult to stand. Automobile drivers notice the shaking. Hanging objects quiver. Furniture breaks. Weak chimneys break. Loose bricks, stones, tiles, cornices, unbraced parapets, and architectural ornaments fall from buildings. Damage to masonry D; some cracks in masonry C. Waves seen on ponds. Small slides along sand or gravel banks. Large bells ring. Concrete irrigation ditches damaged.

VIII General fright; signs of panic. Steering of vehicles is affected. Stucco falls; some masonry walls fall. Some twisting and falling of chimneys, factory stacks, monuments, towers, and elevated tanks. Frame houses move on foundations if not bolted down. Heavy damage to masonry D; damage and partial collapse of masonry C. Some damage to masonry B, none to masonry A. Decayed piles break off. Branches break from trees. Flow or temperature of water in springs and wells may change. Cracks appear in wet ground and on steep slopes.

IX General panic. Damage to well-built structures; much interior damage. Frame structures are racked and, if not bolted down, shift off foundations. Masonry D destroyed; heavy damage to masonry C, sometimes with complete collapse; masonry B seriously damaged. Damage to foundations. Serious damage to reservoirs; underground pipes broken. Conspicuous cracks in the ground. In alluvial soil, sand and mud is ejected; earthquake fountains occur and sand craters are formed.

X Most masonry and frame structures destroyed with their foundations. Some well-built wooden structures and bridges destroyed. Serious damage to dams, dikes, and embankments. Large landslides. Water is thrown on banks of canals, rivers, and lakes. Sand and mud are shifted horizontally on beaches and flat land. Rails bent slightly.

XI Most masonry and wood structures collapse. Some bridges destroyed. Large fissures appear in the ground. Underground pipelines completely out of service. Rails badly bent.

XII Damage is total. Large rock masses are displaced. Waves are seen on the surface of the ground. Lines of sight and level are distorted. Objects are thrown into the air.

[1]At intensity I there may be effects from very large earthquakes at considerable distance in the form of long-period motion. These effects include disturbed birds and animals, swaying of hanging objects, and slow swinging of doors, although people will not feel the shaking and will not recognize the effects as being caused by an earthquake.

[2]Each earthquake effect is listed in the table at the level of intensity at which it appears frequently. It may be found less frequently or less strongly at the preceding (lower) level and more frequently and more strongly at higher levels.

[3]The quality of masonry or brick construction was categorized by Richter (1956) as follows: *Masonry A.* Good workmanship, mortar, and design; reinforced, especially laterally, and bound together by using steel, concrete, etc.; designed to resist lateral forces. *Masonry B.* Good workmanship and mortar; reinforced, but not designed in detail to resist lateral forces. *Masonry C.* Ordinary workmanship and mortar; no extreme weaknesses like failing to tie in at corners, but neither reinforced nor designed against horizontal forces. *Masonry D.* Weak materials, such as adobe; poor mortar; low standards of workmanship; weak horizontally.

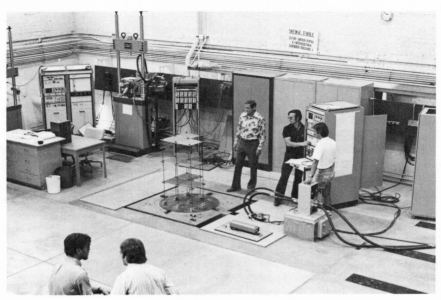

Research on the effects of earthquakes on structures is conducted in university laboratories like the John A. Blume Earthquake Engineering Center at Stanford. The lab contains a shake table that reproduces earthquake ground motion, as well as a data processing and computer facility, Fourier analyzer, and laser interferometer.

this may have been a natural approach, it is, of course, very misleading. The amount of damage depends greatly upon the distance to the hypocenter and upon local factors such as the quality of construction and the soil conditions. Today we refer to the degree of damage at a particular location as the *intensity*, and we measure it by numerical scales. Each earthquake has only one Richter magnitude, but it may produce several intensities, varying from a high intensity in the most heavily damaged region down to the lowest intensity (no damage) far from the epicenter.

To appreciate the concept of intensity, imagine that you are inside a store, talking to the clerk, when suddenly you feel a strong jolt and the floor shakes violently. You are unable to stay on your feet, and around you the shelves tip over, the plate glass windows break, and one side wall collapses with a tremendous roar of falling bricks. Miraculously, you remain unhurt, although others in nearby buildings are not so fortunate. You have experienced intensity IX on the Modified Mercalli intensity scale (or MM scale), which is the scale commonly used in the United States. It is possible that you felt an earthquake of magnitude 6.0 very close by or an earthquake of magnitude 8.0 many kilometers away. Another person, in a different city, might have experienced much milder effects. For instance, he might have heard some creaking in the building, a door rattling, and glassware clinking in the cupboard. At his location, the intensity was only IV, although it was caused by the same earthquake with the same magnitude.

A simplified and edited version of the MM scale is given in Table 5-2. Note that the intensity is stated in Roman numerals, which avoids confusion with magnitude, and that the scale goes only from I to XII. The original scale came into existence in 1902, when it was proposed by Giuseppi Mercalli of Italy and subsequently called the Mercalli scale. In 1931 it was updated and revised by H.O. Wood and F. Neumann of the Caltech Seismological Laboratory and called the Modified Mercalli scale. Then in 1956 Richter further revised the scale and called it the Modified Mercalli scale, 1956 version. Other intensity scales currently in use are the Japan Meteorological Agency (JMA) scale, the Russian MSK scale (named for seismologists S.V. Medvedev, W. Sponheuer, and V. Karnik), and the Chinese intensity scale.

The intensity reported for a particular earthquake always refers to the maximum intensity that the earthquake produced. It can generally be assumed that the maximum intensity will be higher for a larger earthquake than for a smaller one, but the correlation between intensity and magnitude is very rough. Many factors besides magnitude and distance influence the intensity. Two earthquakes of the same magnitude, one with a focal depth of 10 kilometers and the other with a focal depth of 30 kilometers, obviously will produce quite different intensities at the ground surface. Also, certain kinds of soil conditions can greatly amplify the ground motion in one region with respect to another, thus creating higher intensities for the same magnitude of earthquake. However, if these conditions are set aside, the correlation between Richter magnitude and maximum MM intensity is approximately as shown in Table 5-3.

Table 5-3
**Approximate Relationship between
Richter Magnitude and Maximum MM Intensity**

Richter Magnitude	Maximum MM Intensity	Typical Effects
2.0 and under	I-II	Not generally felt by people.
3.0	III	Felt indoors by some people; no damage.
4.0	IV-V	Felt by most people; objects disturbed; no structural damage.
5.0	VI-VII	Some structural damage, such as cracks in walls and chimneys.
6.0	VII-VIII	Moderate damage, such as fractures of weak walls and toppled chimneys.
7.0	IX-X	Major damage, such as collapse of weak buildings and cracking of strong buildings.
8.0 and over	XI-XII	Damage total or nearly total.

How Intensity Is Determined

Intensity is not a measured quantity; its determination is entirely subjective. To obtain intensity, people inspect the affected regions, looking at damage to buildings, tanks, roads, canals, hillsides, and anything else that has been altered by the earthquake. In addition, questionnaires are mailed routinely after an earthquake to government employees such as postmasters, National Park Service personnel, Forest Service personnel, and military and weather service observers. They are requested to return the questionnaires to the U.S. Geological Survey, where their observations concerning the earthquake are studied. Then the Survey assigns intensities to various locations.

After intensity values have been assigned, they are plotted on a map of the region. "Contour lines" of equal intensities, called *isoseismal lines*, are then drawn on the map to divide the region into intensity zones. Of course, the drawing of isoseismal lines is only approximate because of the highly subjective nature of the observations. Nevertheless, such an *intensity map* is a very useful way to show the location of the earthquake, the extent of the damaged region, and the effects of local geology. An intensity map for the 1971 San Fernando earthquake is shown in Figure 5-9. Note that the maximum intensity was XI near the epicenter and that the intensities diminished to V within a distance of 40 to 120 kilometers, depending upon direction. The isoseismal lines also show that the earthquake was felt as far away as 400 kilometers (250 miles).

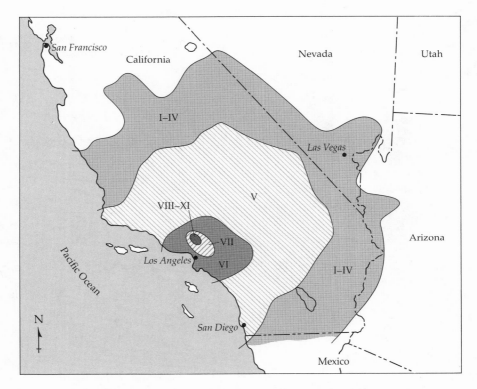

Figure 5-9. Intensity map for the 1971 San Fernando earthquake (magnitude 6.6). The maximum intensity was XI on the Modified Mercalli (MM) scale. The intensity diminished to VI in Los Angeles and V in San Diego.

Can Animals Predict Earthquakes?

(Courtesy of T.O. Sylvester)

6

Earthquake Prediction

The longer it has been since the last one, the closer it is to the next one.

—Professor Richard Jahns,
Department of Geology,
Stanford University

THE IMPLICATIONS OF AN EARTHQUAKE PREDICTION by a government agency are enormous—thousands of lives might be saved if the prediction proved to be accurate, or an entire city might be evacuated to no avail if the prediction proved to be false. Because of the many uncertainties that surround earthquakes, successful predictions have been rare. Nevertheless, the ability to predict accurately is such a desirable goal that today hundreds of scientists, primarily in the United States, Japan, China, and Russia, are engaged in earthquake prediction studies.

The Haicheng, China, Prediction

The world's most famous earthquake prediction took place in 1975 in the city of Haicheng, Liaoning Province, in northeastern China. The region around Haicheng had been under careful study by seismologists for several years before 1975, because there were indications that a large earthquake might take place in the near future. Instruments were installed to record tilting of the land surface, fluctuations in the magnetic field, and changes in the electrical resistance of the ground. The populace was asked to record the water levels in wells and to report any strange behavior of animals.

Instrumental measurements clearly showed that changes were taking place in the earth. By January of 1975 the changes became sufficiently pronounced to justify putting the area on the alert. Preparations were made for taking care of the very old and the very young, emergency instructions were given to workers, and people prepared to sleep out of doors.

By February the signs of an impending earthquake were multiplying. Sudden rises in well-water levels were noted, and scientists stationed at the nearby Yingkou seismological station recorded a dramatic increase in the number of small earthquakes. On the evening of February 3 it was clear to seismologists that a major earthquake could come at any moment, and they so notified local government authorities. Early the next morning an earthquake large enough to be felt (magnitude 4.7) occurred.

On the basis of these events, a general warning was issued at 2:00 in the afternoon. The public was told that an earthquake was expected within the next two days. Disaster relief facilities were mobilized, shops and businesses were closed, hospital patients were moved to temporary shelters, and large numbers of people were evacuated from their buildings. Because it was a bitter cold night, films were shown in the parks and squares to encourage people to stay outside.

Five and a half hours after the warning—at 7:36 P.M.—a large earthquake occurred (magnitude 7.3). Haicheng, a city of 100,000 people, was severely damaged. Hundreds of buildings and factories were destroyed, but because almost everyone was outdoors, the number of deaths was small. It was lucky that the earthquake came so soon after the evacuation; had it occurred a few hours later, many people would have been back indoors to escape the cold.

This remarkable event of February 4, 1975, marked a milestone in earthquake prediction efforts. Although not the first successful prediction, it was the first to predict a large earthquake and the first to save lives, probably thousands of them.

Other Chinese Predictions

One of the earliest predictions in China took place in 1969 near the city of Tianjin (formerly called Tientsin). Workers at the local People's Park, which contains a zoo, began participating in earthquake predictions in 1968. On the morning of July 18, 1969, they were aware of unusual behavior on the part of many of the animals; they said a tiger was depressed, pandas screamed, yaks did not eat, turtles were restless, and swans stayed away from the water. Thinking that these things might be precursors to an earthquake, they reported them to the city's earthquake office. At noon on that day, a magnitude 7.4 earthquake occurred at Bo Hai, the bay to the east of Tianjin. Whether the animal behavior was related to the earthquake or to some local condition, such as the weather, is unknown. Why would these particular animals be affected by the impending earthquake when thousands of others were not?

Three earthquakes in China were successfully predicted in 1976: May 29 in Yunnan Province, August 16 in Sichuan Province (formerly Sze-

The main entrance (top) of the guest house was badly damaged and its rear wing (bottom) collapsed during the 1975 Haicheng, China, earthquake. The city was evacuated only a few hours
before the earthquake; thousands of lives were saved in the world's most successful prediction.
(Courtesy of Dr. Liu Huixian, professor and director of the Institute of Engineering Mechanics,
Academia Sinica, Harbin, China)

chuan), and November 7 in the Sichuan-Yunnan border region. Many months before each earthquake, seismologists had made long-term predictions based on seismicity studies, leveling surveys, and magnetic anomalies. Imminent predictions were issued from a few days to several hours before each earthquake, primarily on the basis of increased numbers of small earthquakes. Emergency preparations were made, and in one case a large-scale evacuation was carried out four days before the earthquake.

Chinese scientists unhesitatingly point out that no predictions were made for many large earthquakes, including the disastrous 1976 Tangshan event, and that the number of false alarms far exceeds the number of successes. As an example, when we talked with seismologists in Xian, the ancient capital famous for its archeological treasures, we learned that a partial evacuation took place a few years earlier, but no earthquake occurred. The official view is that it is better to have many unsuccessful predictions than to allow a major earthquake to go unpredicted. Because the Chinese people have suffered repeatedly from earthquake disasters, they are tolerant of errors in predictions. As far as we can tell, the officials who issue the warnings are not subject to public humiliation nor held liable for losses if they make a mistake.

Predictions in the United States

In the United States a few small earthquakes have been successfully predicted, but none of these predictions resulted in public action. The predictions were important primarily to researchers involved in earthquake studies.

The first successful U.S. prediction was made in 1973 at Blue Mountain Lake in the Adirondack Mountains of upstate New York. In 1972 Columbia University seismologists began measuring seismic wave velocities in the vicinity of the lake, because a few years earlier Russian scientists had observed that changes in wave velocities sometimes preceded earthquakes. Seismic wave velocities are determined by setting off small explosive charges in the ground and measuring the time it takes for the waves to arrive at a nearby location; the speed of wave travel is a physical characteristic of the earth in that particular region. On August 1, 1973, an earthquake prediction was made after sudden changes in wave velocities were observed. The prediction was that an earthquake of magnitude 2.5 to 3.0 would occur within the next few days. In fact, an earthquake of magnitude 2.6 occurred on August 3, so the prediction was successful and created great excitement on the part of seismologists. It provided confirmation of the Russian findings and drew attention to the possibilities for future successful predictions.

Another prediction took place in 1974 near Hollister, California, in the region where the Calaveras fault merges with the San Andreas fault. This region is one of the most heavily instrumented and carefully studied earthquake zones in the world. Data from magnetometers revealed that changes in the earth's magnetic field were taking place, and tiltmeters showed that the ground was moving. Seismologists from the U.S. Geological Survey began studying the area intently, and on November 27, 1974, they met to assess the accumulated data. They concluded that the area was about to have an earthquake, but they were not sufficiently confident to issue a warning to the public. On the day after the meeting, a magnitude 5.2 earthquake occurred. Later they learned that seismic wave velocities had been changing at the same time that the magnetic and tilting changes were occurring. If the seismologists had had the velocity data at the time of their meeting, they undoubtedly would have made a public prediction.

An informal prediction took place in northern California in 1975. The great Oroville earth-fill dam had been completed several years earlier and the reservoir was full by the end of 1968. When the dam was built, seismographs were installed in the vicinity in order to detect any earthquakes that might be generated by the dam and reservoir. Beginning in June 1975 there was a significant increase in seismic activity in a region extending from the dam southward for about fifteen kilometers. Toward the end of July, Professor Bruce Bolt, director of the Seismographic Station at the University of California, Berkeley, thought that the number of small earthquakes was sufficiently alarming to justify a warning of some sort. He phoned Professor George Housner of Caltech, Chairman of the Earthquake Advisory Board of the State of California, who notified the Department of Water Resources. The main Oroville earthquake (magnitude 5.9) came on August 1, so this incident qualifies as a successful, although informal, prediction.

A more formal prediction was made by USGS researchers in 1976. Based upon measurements of creep along the Calaveras fault east of San Jose, California, they predicted in June 1976 that the fault would slip and create an earthquake within a three-month time span centered around January 1, 1977. In fact, a magnitude 3.2 earthquake occurred on December 8, 1976, in the section of the fault that was being studied. Thus, this incident also qualifies as a successful prediction.

From the tentative nature of these predictions, it seems safe to conclude that many more years of study and data acquisition are needed before predictions will be reliable enough to result in community action.

Russian Prediction Efforts

A series of pioneering earthquake prediction studies were conducted in Russia during the 1960s and 1970s. The relationship between changes in seismic wave velocities and the occurrence of earthquakes was first observed in the vicinity of Garm, in Tadzhikistan, during that period. After many years of observations, Soviet seismologists officially predicted on November 1, 1978, that a large earthquake would occur within the next 24 hours in the area around Garm. The prediction was based upon several kinds of evidence, including deformations shown by tiltmeters and strain meters, increases in seismicity, changes in wave velocities, and changes in water wells. One well actually stopped flowing on November 1, and others had sudden drops in flow. An earthquake of magnitude 7.0 came about six hours after the announcement; it was located between the Pamir and Tien Shan Mountains, about 150 kilometers east of Garm. The Russians also report that they have predicted several other earthquakes in Tadzhikistan and Uzbekistan, but few details are available.

Japanese Prediction Efforts

In Japan, comprehensive research on earthquake prediction has been under way since 1964, the year of the destructive Niigata earthquake. Because Japan averages a damaging earthquake every year, there is great public interest in the success of this research.

Some important experiments were carried out between the years 1965 and 1967, when thousands of small earthquakes occurred around the town of Matsushiro in Nagano Prefecture in central Honshu. As many as 600 earthquakes were felt in one day, including some that were large enough to cause damage (magnitude 4 to 5). Changes in the tilt of the ground were observed before the larger earthquakes, which also were preceded by an increase in the number of small earthquakes. Leveling surveys showed considerable uplift of the land, and magnetometers recorded an increase in magnetic intensity. Such observations gave hints as to how earthquakes could be predicted, but successful predictions still await more reliable correlations.

Since 1974 the Tokai region south of Tokyo has been identified as the area where the next great earthquake is most likely to occur. This geographic region includes all of Shizuoka Prefecture and parts of Aichi, Gifu, Kanagawa, Nagano, and Yamanashi Prefectures. The population density is high and industrial activity is heavy. The area has been subjected to great earthquakes in the past (the last one was in 1854), and it has recently been identified as a seismic gap (see later discussion). The region is now the subject of intense seismological study.

In 1978 the Japanese government passed the Large-Scale Earthquake Countermeasures Act, which authorizes a major program of prediction and preparedness. The Japan Meteorological Agency (JMA) was assigned the task of predicting the expected Tokai earthquake. New seismographic stations have been established throughout the region to monitor earth movements, crustal strains, tilting of the surface, changes in gravity, radon emission, and changes in ground water levels. In addition, the number of small earthquakes is being recorded. From all of these observations, the Japanese hope to obtain sufficient data to predict the earthquake. Along with the prediction program, a massive preparedness and educational program is also in progress.

An Aborted Prediction

In January 1981 two U.S. scientists, one from the Bureau of Mines and the other from the U.S. Geological Survey, predicted that three large earthquakes would occur off the coasts of Peru and northern Chile in June, August, and September of 1981. The Richter magnitudes of these earthquakes were predicted as 8.5, 9.4, and 9.9. The latter two numbers were sufficient to cast doubt upon the reliability of the predictions, inasmuch as the largest recorded earthquakes anywhere in the world had magnitudes of 8.9. Nevertheless, the predictions alarmed Peruvian government officials and created a flurry of publicity.

Shortly after the predictions were made, a 12-member panel of U.S. experts, known as the National Earthquake Prediction Evaluation Council, was convened to hear the evidence for the prediction. After two days of hearings, they concluded that no scientific basis existed for the predictions, and they notified the Peruvian government to that effect. As it happened, there were no large earthquakes off the coasts of Peru and northern Chile in 1981. The largest South American earthquake in 1981 occurred off the coast of central Chile near Valparaiso on October 15 and had a magnitude of 7.2; one person was killed in an auto accident by a panicked driver. However, even if there had been a great earthquake farther north, the Council would have called it a coincidence because there was no valid evidence to support the predictions.

Suppose We Have an Official Prediction

Imagine that the U.S. Geological Survey announces a very high probability of a major earthquake along the San Andreas fault near Los Angeles in the next few weeks. It is expected that the earthquake will be capable of causing widespread destruction to buildings, dams, and other structures and that the loss of life may be as high as 2,000. What should be done?

If earthquakes could be predicted with perfect accuracy as to location, time of occurrence, and size, there would be no difficulty in answering this question. People in the affected region would immediately begin preparations, and as the time drew near everyone would move out of doors or to a safe place. Deaths and injuries could be kept to almost zero, although losses to property would still be great. The public would willingly accept whatever inconveniences were involved.

In reality, all predictions will have a high degree of uncertainty. Even the hypothetical prediction stated above is approximate—the location is vague and includes a region many miles in extent, the time period is many days in duration, and the size includes a magnitude range from 6 to 8. Furthermore, the predicted earthquake may not take place at all. Under such conditions, it is not clear what should be done. We can sympathize even now with elected officials who will be forced to make decisions, either for action or inaction, under conditions of great uncertainty—and then will be condemned unmercifully, and perhaps even sued, for having done the wrong thing when their decisions do not accord with subsequent events.

The kinds of actions that can be taken in response to a prediction are many and varied. If there is enough time, buildings can be strengthened, weak structures can be torn down, water levels in reservoirs can be lowered, people can be trained for rescue work and first aid, and those who are unable to care for themselves can be relocated to safer areas. Other actions, requiring less lead time, include the mobilization of emergency personnel; stockpiling of emergency supplies (food, water, medical supplies, etc.); preparation of facilities for refugees; closure of hazardous buildings, bridges, and streets; removal of fragile or dangerous items from shelves; shut-down of dangerous operations in factories or laboratories; and the evacuation of people from unsafe areas, such as below weak dams.

A prediction carrying the weight of a responsible government agency, such as the U.S. Geological Survey, could have serious consequences in the affected region. Great social and economic disruption for society, not to mention personal inconvenience and hardship, could result. Consider what might happen to property values, insurance rates, plans for new construction, job opportunities, and business activity in general. Many residents might move away from the area, and a serious economic recession could result. These consequences may be appropriate if the earthquake really comes, but suppose it doesn't. Was the economic loss justified simply because an earthquake *might* have occurred? This is the kind of question that must be answered as earthquake prediction grows slowly from a guessing game to a scientific methodology.

Unfortunately, the public rarely understands the probabilistic nature of earthquake predictions; science is expected to provide clear-cut answers, not answers fraught with uncertainty. Under these conditions, most scientists believe that the best approach is to release whatever information they have. Even if they tried to withhold data because they thought it would be misinterpreted by the public, they would be unable to prevent information leaks. Furthermore, the withholding of information about an impending earthquake, even though the prediction is highly unreliable, might give insiders an unfair advantage. For example, there might be opportunities for buying or selling property or relocating businesses.

Statistical Predictions

Let us now examine the kinds of evidence that seismologists use to make predictions—statistical data, seismic gaps, and precursors. Then we will turn to the not-so-scientific aspects of prediction, including triggering theories, superstitious beliefs, and animal behavior.

The oldest and most common method for predicting earthquakes is a statistical method based upon an analysis of the earthquake history of the region—the number of earthquakes, their sizes, and how often they occur. Assuming that the seismicity of the region doesn't change, we can estimate the probabilities of future earthquakes from such data. Naturally, the longer the time period for which earthquake records are available, the more accurate are such predictions. In California we have earthquake records for approximately 200 years, but in China more than 2,000 years of records are available.

In an attempt to extend the California earthquake record farther back in time, scientists recently turned to the geological record. A fascinating bit of research was done by Dr. Kerry Sieh, now of Caltech but originally a Stanford graduate student working under the direction of Professor Richard Jahns. By trenching across the San Andreas fault in southern California and inspecting the exposed layers of soil and rock, he determined that great earthquakes had occurred eight times in the past 1,200 years, with the average interval between earthquakes being 140 years.

If the frequency at which earthquakes have occurred in the past is known (either from historical records or geological records), one can make generalized statistical statements about the probabilities of earthquakes in the future. For instance, we can say that an earthquake of magnitude 6.0 or greater is expected in California once every ten months, and an earthquake of magnitude 7.0 or greater is expected once every five and a half years.

Statistical predictions are not helpful for predicting earthquakes in a particular place at a particular time; thus, they are of little value in making emergency preparations. On the other hand, they are of great value to engineers who must design structures to last for 50 or 100 years.

Seismic Gaps

Statistical data on past earthquakes have helped to identify those regions along plate boundaries where the probability of an earthquake is relatively high as compared to other regions along those same boundaries. By studying the amount of earthquake activity that has been occurring in past years, seismologists can determine which regions have been slipping (and hence releasing the accumulated strains) and which regions have been relatively "quiet." It is presumed that strains are building up in the quiet zones and that they are the most likely places for earthquakes to occur. A region along a plate boundary where the seismicity has been significantly less than along adjacent segments of the boundary is called a *seismic gap.* The concept of a seismic gap is useful in long-range prediction of earthquakes, but it offers little hope for predicting the time or magnitude of a particular earthquake at a particular location.

Two seismic gaps along the San Andreas fault in California have caused concern in recent years. In the vicinity of San Francisco, the fault has been remarkably free of earthquakes since 1906, and a segment of the fault north of Los Angeles has not had a significant earthquake since the Fort Tejon earthquake in 1857. Consequently, these regions are strong candidates for a large earthquake in the not-too-distant future. By contrast, the central segment of the fault between those regions is creeping slowly and releasing the accumulated strains; this segment has never been known to generate a large earthquake, although many small ones occur there.

Current estimates place the probabilities of a great earthquake in southern California at 40 percent in the next 30 years; in the San Francisco region, the probability is about half as great. For the entire state, the probability is about 50 percent in the next 30 years.

Alaska has also been studied for seismic gaps. The boundary of the Pacific plate along the Aleutian Islands, the Gulf of Alaska, and the coast of the Alaskan panhandle has been extensively examined by seismologists from the Lamont-Doherty Observatory of Columbia University. In 1968 they identified the region along the Fairweather fault, near Sitka, as one of four seismic gaps where earthquakes had not occurred for many decades. Then in 1972 the Sitka earthquake (magnitude 7.6) occurred, releasing the accumulated strain in that region and lending credence to the seismic gap theory.

The dated strips on the map of Alaska (Figure 6-1) represent regions along the plate boundary where earthquakes of recent times have been accompanied by significant plate movement; for instance, the most westerly strip shows the region of slippage during the February 3, 1965, Rat Islands earthquake. Three significant gaps appear on the map, the one of greatest concern being near Cape Yakataga on the northern coast of the Gulf of Alaska.* The last time this area was hit by a major earthquake was in 1899, when two earthquakes of magnitudes greater than 8.0 struck within the same month. The U.S. Geological Survey is closely observing the Yakataga area and recently installed additional seismographs there. Also,

---

* Adapted from McCann, W. R., Pérez, O. J., and Sykes, L. R., "Yakataga Gap, Alaska: Seismic History and Earthquake Potential," *Science,* vol. 27, March 21, 1980, pp. 1309-1314.

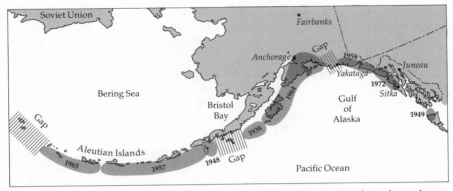

Figure 6-1. Seismic gaps in Alaska. The gaps are regions along the plate boundary where earthquakes have not occurred for many years. These regions are believed to have the highest probabilities for the next earthquake. The gap of greatest concern is in the vicinity of Yakataga. (Adapted from McCann, Pérez, and Sykes)

ground elevations are being measured with a view toward detecting tilts and uplifts.

Seismic gaps have been identified off the coasts of Mexico and Japan, as well as in other places around the world. The Mexican gap was first noted in 1977, and only a year later, on November 29, 1978, the Oaxaca earthquake (magnitude 7.8) took place in precisely the region identified as the gap. Japan has a gap in the Tokai region, as mentioned previously.

Earthquake Precursors

Modern scientific and engineering developments have made it possible to measure a great variety of physical characteristics of the earth, and scientists hope that some of these measurements will make earthquake prediction a reality. Highly accurate and sensitive devices, such as tilt-meters and magnetometers, have been placed in the ground in many places along known fault zones. By monitoring various properties of the earth, seismologists hope to detect correlations between changes in those prop-erties and the occurrence of earthquakes. Any earth characteristics that regularly exhibit changes prior to earthquakes are called *precursors*; the changes themselves are called *anomalies*.

The potential precursors currently under investigation are described briefly on the following pages. All have been observed to change before earthquakes, but not in a consistent manner. Most have resulted in con-tradictions—sometimes changes occurred but no earthquake followed, and sometimes no changes were observed yet there was an earthquake.

Seismicity. The locations and numbers of earthquakes of various mag-nitudes can be an important indicator of impending large earthquakes. For instance, a swarm of small earthquakes often precedes a large earthquake. The detection and counting of earthquakes requires the use of many seismographs and related data-processing facilities. In the United States, this task is performed by the U.S. Geological Survey, the California Division of Mines and Geology, and other agencies.

Crustal movements. Surveys made with the aid of triangulation networks on the ground and observations from satellites in space can detect large-scale deformations, or changes in shape, of the surface of the earth. Measurements at ground level are made with extremely precise surveying instruments equipped with laser light beams. Since resurveying is expensive and time-consuming, many years may elapse between surveys, so that changes in the ground surface may not be detected promptly or dated accurately. Nevertheless, such changes are important indicators of crustal strains.

Subsidence and uplift. Vertical movements in the surface of the land can be measured by precise leveling techniques on land and by tide gauges in the sea. Since the latter are attached to the ground but measure the elevation of the sea, they detect long-term changes in the mean water level, which can be interpreted as an uplift or subsidence of the land itself.

Along the west coast of Honshu Island, Japan, the earth was found to be rising about 2 millimeters per year during the first half of this century. The rising terminated abruptly in the 1964 Niigata earthquake, when the land suddenly dropped as much as 20 centimeters. In California an extensive uplift in the earth's surface along the San Andreas fault northeast of Los Angeles took place during the 1960s and 1970s. Centered in the city of Palmdale, and therefore known popularly as the "Palmdale Bulge," it was 200 kilometers long. The uplift was clearly due to the buildup of strains in the crust, and everyone wondered if it presaged a large earthquake. However, no significant earthquake has yet occurred in that vicinity, and the bulge is subsiding.

Tilting of the land surface. An instrument called a tiltmeter has been developed to measure changes in angle of the ground surface. Tiltmeters are so precise that an instrument in California could measure the tilt of the United States if New York were lifted a mere 5 centimeters (or 2 inches). Tiltmeters usually are installed near fault lines, at depths of 1 or 2 meters below the ground surface. An array of 14 tiltmeters spaced every 6 kilometers (about 4 miles) is located along both sides of the San Andreas fault in the region south of San Juan Bautista; measurements from this array have shown dramatic changes in tilting just prior to small earthquakes.

Strains. The strains in the rocks can be measured by drilling holes and installing strainmeters that measure the relative displacement between two points. Then the strain is determined by dividing the displacement by the distance between the points. These instruments are so sensitive that strains in the earth's crust due to *earth* tides (caused by the gravitational pull of the moon and sun) have been measured. Such earth tides, which are movements in the crust similar to ocean tides, produce changes in land elevations of up to 20 centimeters (8 inches). Creepmeters are similar to strainmeters and are used to measure creep, or slow movement, across fault lines.

Water levels in wells. Underground water levels often rise or fall before earthquakes, as they did at Haicheng, China, presumably because of changes in the strain conditions of the rocks. Earthquakes also have a direct effect on water levels; well water may oscillate from the passage of seismic waves even when the well is at a great distance from the epicenter. Wells located near the epicenter often undergo permanent changes in water level, sometimes becoming higher and sometimes lower.

Wave speeds. The speed of a seismic wave is affected by the strains in the rocks through which the wave travels, as well as by water content and other physical characteristics. To the extent that changes in such physical phenomena are precursors of earthquakes, measurements of changes in wave speed become precursors too. Wave speeds are determined by discharging small amounts of explosives in holes, thus generating seismic waves, and by recording those waves at a nearby location. From the travel times, speeds can be determined. Wave speeds can also be determined from seismograms of actual earthquakes. Because the P and S waves travel at different speeds, the ratio of their speeds may change also. This ratio was first observed to be an earthquake precursor in the Russian experiments near Garm, as previously described.

There are many problems associated with the use of wave speeds to predict earthquakes. It takes hundreds of tests to obtain data clearly showing the changes in speed ratio. Where should such tests be made? Are the results unique to certain regions, or are they typical of earthquakes everywhere? In order to be useful, such tests would have to be conducted at the same location at frequent intervals for many years, so that the changes could be related to an actual earthquake, which might occur once in 20, 50, or 100 years. And so this precursor, like the others, can be said to have promise, but it is far from being a workable tool of earthquake prediction.

Geomagnetism. The earth's magnetic field may undergo localized changes due to strains in the rocks and movements of the crust, and hence magnetometers have been developed to measure minute variations in magnetism. Such changes have been observed prior to earthquakes in most places where magnetometers have been used, including the San Andreas fault zone and China.

Geoelectricity. Changes in the electrical resistance of the earth may possibly be connected with earthquakes, as well as with such other natural phenomena as rainfall (which changes the moisture content of the earth).

Measurements are made by placing electrodes in the ground, a few kilometers apart, and determining the resistance of the earth between them. Most of the electrical conduction is through water in the rocks, hence the resistivity changes when the water content changes. Tests have been conducted along the San Andreas fault near Hollister by USGS scientists, and some correlations with small earthquakes have been noted. In laboratory experiments, electrical resistivity has been observed to change during the period of dilatancy immediately preceding fracture of the rocks.

Radon content of the ground water. Radon is a radioactive gas found in ground and well water. It has a half-life of 3.8 days and is constantly emanating from the earth into the atmosphere. Changes in the radon content of well water were first observed before earthquakes in Russia, where a 10-year increase in the amount of radon dissolved in the water of deep wells was followed by a sharp drop just before the Tashkent earthquake of magnitude 5.3 in 1966.

In the United States, the radon-emission monitoring system now consists of over a hundred stations in central and southern California. In August of 1981 increased levels of radon in several southern California wells were observed; the increases were noticeable enough to provoke considerable speculation about whether they were precursors of an earthquake. As one USGS scientist said at the time, "If a large earthquake were to occur in the near future, then many would claim that there were abundant examples of precursory phenomena." However, no earthquake occurred, so the speculation continues.

At the present time, there simply is not enough accumulated data pertaining to any of the preceding precursory phenomema to provide a basis for reliable earthquake predictions. It will take many years of measurements and numerous earthquakes before that goal is reached. Because it is so expensive to measure a variety of phenomena, and because there are so many different earthquake zones to be monitored (even in the United States), we feel safe in predicting that most earthquakes will not be predicted.

Dilatancy Theory

A theory that may explain some of the precursors comes from laboratory tests performed on rocks subjected to very high strains. Known as the dilatancy theory, it was first conceived by William Brace of MIT in the 1960s, and the concepts were expanded by Amos M. Nur of Stanford in 1972. In this context, dilatancy means an increase in volume of the rocks due to deformation or strains. As crustal movements occur, strains build up in the rocks, eventually producing microscopic cracks. These cracks change the physical properties of the rocks; for example, seismic wave velocities are reduced, volume is increased, and electrical resistivity is altered (increased if the rocks are dry and decreased if they are wet). Also, as water enters the cracks they no longer can be closed up, hence the rocks increase in volume and the ground surface itself may be raised. Eventually, water will diffuse throughout the entire dilated region, raising the pore pressures in the cracks and weakening the rocks. Such changes may lead to an earthquake. The earthquake then releases the built-up strains, water is squeezed out, and the rocks recover many of their original properties.

Triggering Mechanisms

Because the slow movement of the plates causes strains to accumulate very gradually in the crustal rocks, it is logical to consider the possibility of a "triggering" action for earthquakes. A "trigger" is some physical mechanism that initiates failure in the highly strained rocks. For example, a sudden change in stress in the rocks, such as occurs when a reservoir is filled with water, is a possible trigger. Weather patterns might play a role in triggering earthquakes; for instance, we know that the atmospheric pressure on the earth's surface is changed by the passage of a meteorological front. Also, another earthquake is a potential trigger, because it creates seismic waves and causes the earth to vibrate. Unfortunately, there is not enough evidence at the present time to use any of these phenomena for predicting earthquakes.

A possible triggering mechanism is the action of tides caused by the moon and sun. We know that tides exist not only in the oceans but also in the solid crust, but no one knows whether the effects are large enough to trigger earthquakes. James Berkland, a geologist with the County of Santa Clara in California, has been the principal proponent of the idea that earth and ocean tides serve as triggers. He coined the phrase "seismic window" for the time periods when he believed earthquakes were most likely to occur as the result of being triggered by tidal strains in the earth's crust. A window is taken to be the eight-day period following syzygy, which in this case is the alignment of the sun, earth, and moon. Syzygies occur whenever there is a new or full moon; at such times the earth's crust undergoes maximum tidal deformation. The seismic-window theory has been tested by comparing the times of hundreds of past earthquakes with the tides, but according to USGS investigators, no correlation has yet been observed.

While it seems plausible that the stresses and deformations in the earth due to the gravitational pull of the sun and the moon could trigger earthquakes, it seems not only implausible but ridiculous to think that planets could serve as triggers. The combined gravitational pull of all the other planets together is but a hundred-thousandth of the gravitational pull of the sun and moon. In the years 1981 and 1982, a syzygy occurred in which Saturn, Jupiter, Venus, Mars, the sun, and the earth were nearly lined up, an event that occurs about once every 180 years. No increase in earthquake activity occurred during those years, which was no surprise to seismologists. Unfortunately, publicity is sometimes generated from such improbable notions as "the Jupiter effect." The authors of a 1974 book by that name expressed little doubt that "the planetary and solar influence in the early 1980s, following the rare planetary alignment, will provide that trigger. In particular, the Los Angeles region will, we believe, be subjected to the most massive earthquake experienced by a major center of population during this century." Elsewhere in their book, the authors said, "in 1982 . . . Los Angeles will be destroyed." It is our guess that the principal "Jupiter effect" was to create publicity and profit for the prophets.

There is an obvious reason why any theory that attempts to predict earthquakes on the basis of just one phenomenon, whether that phenomenon is the tide, the weather, an astronomical event, magnetism, elapsed time since the last earthquake, or anything else, is doomed to failure. Earthquakes are extremely complicated physical actions that are related to plate movement, strength of rocks, local geology, groundwater conditions, and dozens of other factors that are different at every place on earth. Because the occurrence of an earthquake is the result of a combination of many such factors, its statistical correlation with any one factor is bound to be extremely low.

Superstitious Beliefs

Throughout the centuries, numerous legends and superstitious beliefs have surrounded earthquakes and their prediction. People have always feared earthquakes and we can readily understand why primitive man felt the need to explain them in terms of the supernatural. However, in the light of today's understanding of geologic processes, there is no excuse for intelligent people to be misled by quacks. Individuals claiming special powers for themselves have prophesied earthquakes since time immemorial, just as they have other disasters, and even the end of the world. In fact, there is no correlation between such predictions and actual earthquakes. Someone predicts a great California earthquake every few months, and, of course, someday the prediction will be correct. However, the principal effect of such predictions is to mislead the gullible. Knowing that the lucky predictor will be granted both fame and credibility provides ample incentive for people to keep on predicting.

Animal Behavior

For centuries unusual animal behavior before earthquakes has been reported, although until recently the reports always came after the earthquakes, not before. There is no way to tell whether the behavior was actually related to earthquakes or was merely behavior of the kind that occurs every day somewhere in the vicinity, especially since the reports range from things that supposedly happened a few minutes before an earthquake to those that happened several days in advance. Another difficulty has been the general unreliability of the reports—often they were second-hand, and often they turned out to be descriptions of animal behavior during or after the earthquake, not before.

It is quite possible that animals can sense phenomena, such as changes in magnetic or electrical fields, that human beings cannot sense. Also, they may be able to detect small tremors that would go unnoticed by people. Of course, modern instruments can detect all such changes, but instruments are relatively new and are located in only a few places around the world.

One of the obvious difficulties in trying to use animal behavior to predict earthquakes is that there are so many possible causes of unusual behavior, including weather conditions, food, and health. Only if there are widespread changes in behavior patterns for which no other cause is available would one feel confident in using animal reactions for predicting earthquakes.

Research on animal behavior is currently being undertaken in the United States and elsewhere. The USGS is systematically collecting reports of unusual behavior, in the hope that some conclusions will emerge. In China, people are encouraged to report any strange animal behavior to their local earthquake office. It is said that animal behavior was a factor in predicting the 1975 Haicheng earthquake, although there is no doubt that the most important precursors were measured instrumentally. Chinese seismologists have made it clear that predictions are not made unless several lines of evidence all point to an impending earthquake.

In 1980 the writers had an opportunity to visit China for the purpose of discussing earthquake engineering. We met with many engineering groups, gave lectures, asked questions, and visited Tangshan, the city that was destroyed in the 1976 earthquake. Naturally, we inquired about earthquake prediction at every opportunity. At Tangshan we learned that a long-term warning had been issued many months before the earthquake. However, the actual earthquake came unexpectedly, without foreshocks, and was much stronger (magnitude 7.8) than anyone would have predicted for that region. When we inquired of survivors about animal behavior, we were told stories like these: A family in a building heard dogs crying, water birds flying, and insects buzzing shortly before the earthquake; another person heard a donkey crying in the middle of the night, prior to the earthquake; and someone heard a horse and a cow cry about an hour before the large aftershock. All of these stories were related to us second- or thirdhand; none of the people we talked to had any such experiences to relate. It seemed to us that these animal stories were not unusual and could be ordinary daily events having no relationship to the earthquake. Furthermore, considering the thousands of farm animals in and around Tangshan, it is surprising that the animal stories were so few and so vague.

When we asked one of the leading Chinese earthquake specialists about animal behavior as a predictor of earthquakes, he said he gave it no credence, although he went on to say that peasants living in the countryside tended to believe in it. It was our observation that seismologists in China use the same techniques for prediction as are used elsewhere.

Are Predictions the Answer?

To show the current status of earthquake prediction, consider two recent damaging earthquakes in California. The 1983 Coalinga earthquake (magnitude 6.5) was a surprise to everyone, scientists and public alike, yet Coalinga is located in the part of central California where geologic and seismologic knowledge is the most complete. The story of the 1971 San Fernando earthquake (magnitude 6.6) is similar—it occurred at a time and place that no one expected. The May 1983 earthquake of magnitude 7.7 near Akita, Japan, is another example. Japanese earthquake-preparedness programs have concentrated on the Tokai region, south of Tokyo, where everyone agrees a great earthquake is impending. The Akita earthquake, in northwest Japan, caught people unprepared; it did much damage and killed 106 people. From these examples, and from what we have described about precursors in this chapter, it seems clear that dependable and useful predictions will not come for many years, if ever.

Then why are we so interested in predictions? After all, it is misleading to think that successful predictions will solve earthquake problems for us. A successful prediction will not avert the earthquake; the earthquake can still cause much damage to buildings and facilities. Furthermore, even if we have a reliable prediction, is the evacuation of cities such as San Francisco and Los Angeles really feasible?

The best way to reduce losses from earthquakes is to prepare for them. We can prepare in many ways, such as improving disaster facilities, educating the public, and improving the level of engineering design and construction. However, the single most important step in preparation is to strengthen old buildings so that they will not collapse or suffer extensive damage. This is a much better way to save lives than evacuating a city. Indeed, who wants to return to a ruined city after a successful evacuation?

As Richter himself said a few years ago, "I regret the pervasive emphasis on prediction. It directs attention away from the known risks and the known measures that could be taken to remove them. We know where the dangers are and which structures in those areas are unsafe."

So let's turn next to the engineering aspects of earthquakes.

The Agua Caliente bridge on the highway between Guatemala City and El Progreso collapsed during the 1976 earthquake, hindering rescue work for many cities and villages. (Photo by Robert W. Madden, courtesy National Geographic Society)

7

Engineering Design

If a builder builds a house for a man and does not make its construction firm and the house collapses and causes the death of the owner of the house—that builder shall be put to death. If it destroys property, he shall restore whatever it destroyed, and because he did not make the house firm he shall rebuild the house which collapsed at his own expense. If a builder builds a house for a man and does not make its construction meet the requirements and a wall falls—that builder shall strengthen the wall at his own expense.
—The Code of Hammurabi, c. 2250 B.C.

AS THE POPULATION of the United States increases and urbanization spreads, the potential for a major earthquake catastrophe grows alarmingly. Consider the San Francisco Bay Area: At the time of the great 1906 earthquake its population was about 0.5 million; today, it is 5 million and still increasing. In 1906, the population of the entire state of California was only 2 million; today, it is over 24 million.

A growing population requires more buildings, dams, roads, bridges, canals, pipelines, power plants, and communication systems—collectively termed the *infrastructure* of society. In California, mile after mile of formerly fertile farmland, relatively immune to earthquake damage, is now covered by such construction. An earthquake of magnitude 7.5 or higher in metropolitan Los Angeles or San Francisco could kill from 2,000 to 20,000 people, injure thousands more, destroy billions of dollars worth of property, and cause incalculable social and economic disruption.

The engineering challenge is to design and build the infrastructure so as to minimize these losses. With proper engineering design, structures can be built that will withstand the most extreme ground shaking and will not collapse. However, *complete* protection from damage is an unrealistic goal, because society is unwilling to pay the costs. We accept a certain degree of risk in our structures, just as we do in other aspects of our lives, such as transportation.

In assessing the potential for losses from future earthquakes, we must recognize that losses result from a combination of risks and hazards. *Risks* represents everything that we have to lose—including both life and property. The risk is high in areas of dense population; it is low in an open field in the country, where there is little that can be damaged. *Hazards* represents those natural events that threaten life and property; examples are earthquakes, landslides, tornadoes, fires, and floods. In short, hazards are the sources of danger, and risks are the potential losses that those sources might generate.

The combination of risks and hazards determines the probability of losses in any particular region. Consider these examples: A poorly constructed apartment building crowded with occupants represents a high risk, but if it is located in a low-hazard area (where earthquakes are virtually unknown), the probability of losses from earthquakes is extremely small. Now reverse the elements; a strong, well-constructed and sparsely occupied garage building, even if it is situated in a highly seismic area, represents a low probability of losses. But place the weak apartment building near the San Andreas fault and the likelihood of losses becomes alarmingly high.

Earthquake Hazards

The earthquake hazard is usually represented on *seismic hazard maps*, such as the map of the United States shown in Figure 7-1. It is no surprise that the most hazardous zones (the darker the shading, the greater the hazard) are in the western states and that California has the most serious problems because its huge metropolitan areas—Los Angeles, San Francisco, Oakland, San Jose and San Diego—are located in regions of high seismicity. It is less well known that many areas of the eastern United States are also classified as seismic, particularly the central Mississippi River valley and the region around Charleston, South Carolina. Of course, when considered as a whole, the eastern part of the country is clearly less hazardous than the western part. But the lower hazard in the East is partially countered by higher risk—buildings generally are older and were

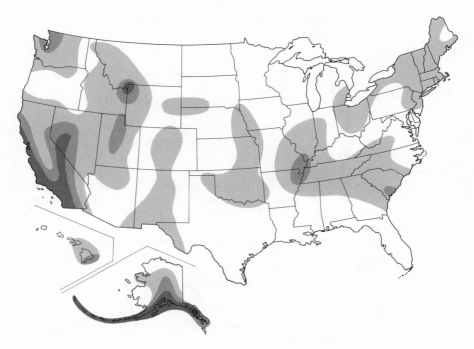

Figure 7-1. Major earthquake zones of the United States. The regions of highest seismicity are denoted by the darkest shading. Approximately 70 million people live in areas where the earthquake hazard is significant.

designed with lower earthquake requirements (or no earthquake requirements), so that a potential for significant losses still exists. In the entire country, about 70 million people live in regions where the earthquake hazard is significant.

Levels of seismic hazard are determined largely by the frequency and size of known earthquakes and by geologic conditions. The longer the historical record, the more accurately we can assess the hazard. The record of earthquakes in China spans more than 2,000 years, but in the United States we must work with a relatively short history—about 300 years in the East and about 200 years in California. It is especially difficult to assign probabilities for the occurrence of major earthquakes when the time span is so short, because large earthquakes are separated by long time intervals. In California the historical records have recently been supplemented by geologic investigations, as discussed in Chapter 6.

In addition to the historical record of earthquakes, geologic conditions have a major role in determining the seismic hazard. For example, the existence of a major plate boundary in California would indicate a high seismic hazard even if the historical earthquake record covered only a few

Table 7-1
Important Elements in Reducing Earthquake Losses

Pre-earthquake
- Engineering design of structures
    Buildings must be designed to resist the earthquake forces.
- Strengthening of existing structures
    Old and weak structures must be upgraded to provide safety against collapse.
- Building codes
    Well-conceived codes must be adopted and enforced as a means of safeguarding the public.
- Land-use planning and zoning
    Seismic hazards, including active faults, landslide potential, and liquefaction potential must be considered when deciding upon proper use of land areas.
- Disaster preparedness
    Emergency services must be developed and disaster plans must be prepared.
- Public education and training
    People must understand the nature of earthquakes and be prepared for them.
- Earthquake insurance
    Insurance must be available to provide financial protection against major losses.
- Predictions and warnings
    Even generalized predictions provide notice that we should begin preparations.

Post-earthquake
- Emergency services
    Prompt services by qualified personnel must be available to provide care for the injured, control fires, reduce crime, and restore community life.
- Self-sufficiency on the part of individuals and small groups
    People must be prepared not only to take care of themselves but also to care for others.
- Engineering and construction services
    These services provide the ability to recover quickly and restore facilities.
- Financial assistance
    Government aid may be needed so that the burden of the disaster is shared by the entire population.
- Social assistance and psychological counseling
    Community organizations can provide support for individuals and groups; counseling can help those who suffer psychological problems as a result of the disaster.

years and included no large earthquakes. The same can be said for the presence of well-defined faults in Nevada, Utah, Idaho, and Alaska and active volcanoes in Hawaii.

In the eastern United States, where earthquakes are infrequent and active faults are not in evidence, the level of seismic hazard must be assigned on the basis of relatively scanty evidence. The New Madrid earthquakes of 1811 and 1812, for instance, are the main reason for classifying the region along the central Mississippi River as an area of high seismic hazard. For Charleston, South Carolina, the earthquake of 1886 is the reason, even though the occurrence of a single major earthquake is hardly a reliable basis for assigning a high degree of seismicity to an area. For all we know, the Charleston earthquake may not be repeated for thousands of years; perhaps the next major earthquake on the eastern seaboard will hit New York or Philadelphia, not Charleston.

Research on hazard analysis is currently in progress at several government agencies and universities, including Stanford, and seismic hazard maps are updated frequently. Their importance lies in the fact that engineers use them to determine the degree of seismic resistance that must be built into a structure.

Loss Reduction

We can do little to diminish earthquake hazards, but we can do much to reduce risks and thereby reduce losses. Earthquake engineers have a crucial role in this process, because they are both structural designers and earthquake specialists. Builders, architects, planners, owners, and government officials—anyone who is involved in the building process—can also be instrumental in reducing risks. Builders must adhere to high standards of materials and workmanship; architects and planners must make sure that buildings are not constructed in hazardous areas such as fault zones, steep hillsides, and mudflats; owners must repair and strengthen old buildings and must properly brace the contents; and government officials must enact and enforce regulations governing seismic safety. Losses are also reduced when communities maintain adequate emergency services (medical, fire, and police) to cope with disasters.

Some of the factors that are important for reducing earthquake losses are listed in Table 7-1.

Good Construction Makes a Difference

The importance of good engineering practices and high standards in construction is evident if we compare the effects of two very similar earthquakes—the 1971 San Fernando, California, earthquake and the 1972 Managua, Nicaragua, earthquake, with magnitudes of 6.6 and 6.2, respectively. Both earthquakes occurred at times of day when most people were

The first floor of the U.S. Embassy building in Managua, Nicaragua, completely collapsed beneath the second floor in the 1972 earthquake.

at home, and in both cases the population of the strongly shaken area was approximately 1 million. But there was an important difference: the San Fernando earthquake affected buildings that were relatively new and had been designed under a building code that included earthquake requirements, whereas the Managua earthquake affected an older city in which very few buildings had been designed to meet modern requirements.

This difference in construction led to markedly different human and economic effects. The San Fernando earthquake caused 58 deaths and $550 million in economic losses, with very little long-term social or economic disruption. In Managua, more than 5,000 people died, and the economic loss was comparable to the annual gross national product of the entire country. The disruption of the nation's capital city and economic center had serious social and political consequences; today, many years after the earthquake, the reconstruction of Managua and the rebuilding of the economy are still not complete.

In the Tangshan, China, earthquake of 1976, the entire city of a million people was destroyed and more than 240,000 people were killed. None of the buildings existing in Tangshan before the earthquake were designed to resist seismic forces; the most common type of construction had unreinforced brick walls, which readily fell down during the ground shaking.

Earthquake Engineering

In recent years our knowledge of earthquakes and their effects has grown tremendously. Each new earthquake brings to structural engineers a wealth of recorded data on the characteristics of ground shaking and the dynamic response of buildings to that shaking. *Earthquake engineering* has emerged as an important new specialty within civil engineering. Earthquake engineers are specialists in the planning and design of structures and facilities in seismic regions. Their work requires not only a knowledge of structural engineering, but also a knowledge of soils, rocks, and materials of construction. They must understand the mechanisms of earthquakes, the nature of the ground motion, and how that motion will affect a structure. Subspecialties are now developing within earthquake engineering; for instance, some earthquake engineers specialize in hazard analysis and others specialize in the design of critical structures, such as dams or power plants.

How earthquake engineers use their knowledge is largely determined by the needs of the country. The fundamental goal of earthquake engineering—to minimize loss of life, injuries, and damage—has to be achieved within the standards of quality set by society at large. Such standards are usually set indirectly and depend upon economic capabilities. In China, an economic factor is written into the building codes; when the economy is good, standards of construction are higher; when it is poor, standards are lower.

Even the most prosperous societies cannot afford to construct all buildings so that they will survive a strong earthquake with no damage. Some level of risk must be accepted. That level is established through experience, just as it is in ordinary activities of daily life, such as flying in an airplane, sleeping in a hotel, or driving a car. Additional electronic monitoring of the movement of planes would reduce the number of collisions; smoke detectors in every hotel room would provide earlier detection of fires; and air bags in automobiles would reduce the number of deaths and injuries. But each such reduction in risk carries a price tag, and we collectively decide how much we are willing to pay for less risk. So it is with building design and construction—higher resistance to earthquake damage costs money. The trade-off becomes evident whenever a community tries to enact an ordinance requiring that old, weak buildings be upgraded; the principal objectors are the building owners who must pay the costs.

Based upon past experience in determining the level of risk that society accepts, earthquake engineers have established design criteria that may be stated informally as follows:

- In small earthquakes (magnitudes less than 5.5), buildings should suffer little or no damage

- In moderate earthquakes (magnitudes between 5.5 and 7.0), some damage is acceptable but the buildings should be repairable
- In large earthquakes (magnitudes greater than 7.0), buildings should protect lives and should not collapse, although they may have to be demolished later

More stringent requirements are imposed for emergency facilities such as hospitals, fire stations, police stations, and emergency operations centers that must remain functional after an earthquake. The standards for dams and power plants (thermal and nuclear) are so strict that the most advanced knowledge of engineers, geologists, and seismologists—and many years of effort—must be brought to bear on their design and construction.

Engineering Design

Design of buildings has two distinct aspects—architectural design is concerned with appearance and function, and engineering design is concerned with structure and strength. Of course, the two aspects are intimately related, and engineers and architects work together when designing a building. An exception is a single-family dwelling, which normally does not require an engineer because its structural design is handled with the aid of specifications and tabulated data. Other types of structures, such as bridges, dams, and towers, are designed solely by engineers.

The visible part of a building, that is, the part above ground, is called the *superstructure*. Below ground is the *foundation*, which may have any of a variety of forms (such as footings, walls, slabs, piles, caissons) and may cost as much as the superstructure. To design a foundation properly, the engineer must have a detailed knowledge of the soil and geologic conditions at the site; this information is obtained by drilling holes into the ground and taking samples of the materials.

The superstructure consists of the structural support system, which is what holds the building up, plus the walls, roofs, partitions, utilities, elevators, stairs, water tanks—everything not part of the foundation. The structural system may be a steel frame consisting of beams, girders, and columns; or a reinforced concrete frame consisting of columns and floor slabs; or a series of bearing walls with horizontal floor diaphragms; or any of numerous other arrangements. Sometimes shear walls are used, either alone or with a frame. A shear wall is a large, rigid wall of reinforced concrete or reinforced masonry that extends for the height of the building and resists the horizontal earthquake forces. Shear walls create a relatively rigid structure; steel frames produce a flexible structure. Properly designed, both systems are capable of resisting earthquake loads.

The loads acting on a structure consist of the weight of the structure itself (called *dead load*) and the superimposed loads (called *live loads*). Live loads are the weight of the contents of the building (such as people, furnishings, computers, machinery, stored goods, and water supplies); snow on a roof; wind pressure (and wind suction) on walls and roofs; impact loads from vehicles or machinery; and, of course, earthquake loads. All except the earthquake loads are direct physical actions—they push or pull on the structure, sometimes vertically and sometimes horizontally. Earthquake loads are distinctly different from the others; in a strict sense they are not really loads at all. Instead, what happens is this: When the ground moves under the structure, it causes the structure to shake and vibrate in a very irregular manner. This action is similar to the effect of a horizontal force acting on the structure, hence the phrase "earthquake loads."

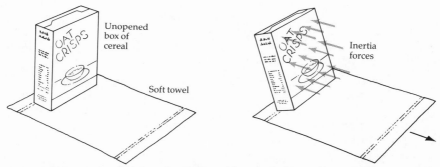

Figure 7-2. Inertia forces. When the towel is pulled to the right, the box falls to the left. The box acts as if it were being pushed to the left by horizontal inertia forces; these inertia forces are the kinds of loads that act on a building during an earthquake.

To understand the nature of earthquake loads, try a simple experiment. Place a box of breakfast cereal on a soft towel lying on a table; then pull suddenly on the towel (Figure 7-2). If the pull is to the right, the box falls to the left, as if it were being pushed to the left by an unseen force. There is no actual push, of course. Instead, because of its mass, the box possesses inertia that tends to resist any motion. Therefore, when the towel moves to the right, the box tries to stay put, which means that it must fall to the left. Engineers speak of fictitious "inertia forces" that are developed in the box when the towel moves. A similar process is at work when the ground moves under a building or other structure. However, the process is much more complex because earthquake ground motion is not as simple as the one-directional movement of the towel.

During an earthquake, the ground moves simultaneously in three mutually perpendicular directions. Furthermore, in all three directions the motion is back and forth in a seemingly random manner, as shown by the typical seismogram in Figure 5-5 (p. 72). We must emphasize, however, that a single seismogram gives only one component of the motion. The actual motion is obtained by superimposing three seismograms in three perpendicular directions. As the ground moves in this extremely complicated manner, inertia forces are created throughout the mass of the structure. It is these forces that cause the building to move and damage to occur.

To design a building to support its own weight and that of its contents is relatively easy, because these loads can be predicted accurately and do not change appreciably. We say that they are *static* loads. As we have seen, earthquake loads are *dynamic*, in that they change rapidly during the earthquake—not only do they vary in magnitude from zero to large values, but they constantly change direction. Furthermore, it is impossible to predict in advance how they are going to vary, because every earthquake exhibits different characteristics. Nevertheless, the structural engineer is still required to design a building that will resist these earthquake forces. His task is half science and half art, the latter being a euphemism for acquired skills, informed judgment, intuition, and plain guesswork.

Certain general characteristics help make a building resistant to earthquake effects. An important feature is regularity and symmetry in the overall shape of the building. A building shaped like a box (that is, rectangular both in plan and elevation) is inherently stronger than one that is L-shaped or U-shaped (such as a building with wings). An irregularly shaped building will twist as it vibrates, increasing the damage. We say that it is subjected to *torsion.*

In general, the smaller the openings in a building, the less damage it will suffer in an earthquake. However, this criterion conflicts with the desire for light and openness and with the need for doors and passageways. Thus, compromises between structural and architectural goals must be made. If it is necessary to have large openings through a building, or if an open first floor is desired, then special provisions should be made to ensure structural integrity.

Changes in the structural system of a building from one floor to the next should be avoided. Columns should run continuously from foundation to roof, without interruptions or changes in materials. If shear walls are used, they too should extend from foundation to roof. Dramatic evidence of what happens when this rule is violated was provided by the near collapse of the Olive View Hospital in San Fernando in 1971 and the Imperial County Services Building in El Centro in 1979. In both cases, shear walls were interrupted at the first floor in order to provide an open first floor. The resulting damage was so extensive that both buildings had to be demolished.

Even though the ground failed directly under it, this house still held together during the 1971 San Fernando earthquake. The main part of the house, built like a box, was relatively undamaged but the garage, with a large opening at the front, leaned to the side. This damage represents intensity IX on the Modified Mercalli scale. (Photo by R. Castle, courtesy of USGS)

Ductility in a structure is another desirable feature. By ductility we mean the ability of the structure to bend, sway, and deform by large amounts without collapsing. The opposite condition in a structure is called *brittleness*. Brittleness arises both from the use of materials that are inherently brittle and from the misuse of otherwise ductile materials. Brittle materials crack under loads; some examples are adobe, brick, and concrete blocks. It was no surprise that most of the damage during the May 2, 1983, earthquake in Coalinga was to old unreinforced masonry structures—buildings constructed of brittle materials, poorly tied together. The addition of steel reinforcement can give brittle materials some ductility. Reinforced concrete, for example, can be made ductile by adequate use of reinforcing steel and closely spaced steel ties.

Most people think of steel as a rigid material, but actually it can be pulled and stretched like taffy before it will break. A round bar of structural steel can be twisted through several complete revolutions—so that the surface of the bar looks like a twisted rope—before it will fracture. No steel building has ever collapsed from ground shaking; the bending of a tall steel building during an earthquake can be compared to a palm tree bending in a typhoon.

The most important feature of structural design is encompassed in the

A "tilt-up" panel fell out of the wall of this building during the 1971 San Fernando earthquake. When tilt-up construction is used, the panels must be securely tied to the roof to prevent this type of failure. (Photo by R. Castle, courtesy of USGS)

earthquake engineer's rule: *Tie the structure together*. Even adobe buildings can be made safer by joining the parts with reeds, vines, ropes, or whatever is available. In modern construction, "tying the structure together" means joining the beams, columns, slabs, and walls by strong and ductile connections. Joints in steel frames must be moment-resistant and held with bolts or weldments. In reinforced concrete construction, reinforcing bars and ties must be ample in number; they must be bent around corners and deeply embedded in the concrete. In wood buildings, ample nailing and bolting are necessary. Almost all structural failures during earthquakes have occurred at weak connections, that is, connections where the members were not properly tied together. This rule also applies to bridges; several bridge spans fell during the 1971 San Fernando earthquake because the main deck slabs were not properly tied to the abutments and piers.

Good earthquake-resistant design and construction cannot be taken for granted. Many engineers and architects have received no training in seismic design. Owners are sometimes interested in their buildings only as short-term investments; knowing that damaging earthquakes are infrequent, they don't want to spend money on putting seismic strength into the structure, and they tend to rush the period for design and construction. The fact that as little as 5 percent of the initial cost of a building can make the difference between minimal seismic resistance and a well-built, earthquake-resistant structure may be brushed aside even though strengthening a building at a later date (perhaps in response to public pressure or new

The stair tower of the Olive View Hospital broke away from the main building and crashed through the roof of the lower story during the 1971 San Fernando earthquake. (Courtesy of USGS)

legal requirements) may cost as much as 50 to 100 percent of the original building cost. Furthermore, when an earthquake does come, the owners may not only lose their building but may also be subject to huge claims for injuries or deaths. It is the responsibility of architects and engineers to explain these matters to owners and developers and to convince them of the necessity of building high levels of earthquake resistance into their structures.

Building Codes

Building codes are legal documents adopted by cities and counties to govern construction within their jurisdictions. They contain specifications pertaining to materials and methods of construction, as well as rules and guidelines for engineering design. The purpose of a code is to set *minimum* standards so that buildings will be resistant to fires, earthquakes, and other hazards. However, no code can make a building completely "safe." There are numerous examples of new buildings that were designed under a building code and yet met disaster—recent tragedies were the collapse of a hotel walkway in Kansas City in 1981 (114 deaths), the failure of the Olive View Hospital near San Fernando in 1971, and the destruction of the County Services Building in El Centro in 1979.

The essence of the matter is this: a code sets only minimum standards and cannot cover all eventualities. In reality, the quality of a building depends much more upon the talents of the engineer, the architect, and the builder than it does upon the code. Qualified people, given the time and means, do not need a building code to create good structures that are safe under all conditions that can reasonably be expected to occur. Inexperienced people, especially if pressed to save time and money, may design structures that satisfy the code but perform badly under loads.

In California, the earthquake provisions of building codes are upgraded every few years, especially after damaging earthquakes, so that in spite of some notable exceptions, we can state positively that buildings designed under today's codes are better able to resist ground shaking than buildings designed under older codes (or no codes at all). However, it is still important to emphasize that there is no such thing as an earthquake-proof building. As our mentor, Dr. John Blume, says, "Don't say 'proof' unless you're talking about whiskey."

Earthquake provisions were first introduced into California building codes after the 1906 San Francisco earthquake, although they were carefully disguised as requirements for "wind loads" rather than "earthquake loads." The reason? San Franciscans wanted to play down the earthquake hazard in order to encourage the development of the city. The next major improvement in earthquake codes came immediately after the 1933 Long Beach earthquake, with the passage of the Field and Riley Acts by the state legislature. These acts require that schools and other public buildings meet certain standards for seismic safety. Since then, the legislature has enacted numerous other laws pertaining not only to schools but also to hospitals, dams, and bridges.

The earthquake-engineering provisions of California building codes are based upon recommendations of the Structural Engineers Association of California, which regularly updates its standards in the light of current research and experiences with recent earthquakes. California leads the way in earthquake-engineering research, and the seismic provisions of its codes are generally adopted by other states (and even other countries) with suitable modifications for local conditions.

Strengthening of Existing Structures

Even as we upgrade our building codes and design new structures to higher standards, we must not forget that the major risks to society come from structures built many years ago. Our cities contain large numbers of old one- to ten-story buildings of unreinforced brick masonry, decayed wood, and weak concrete. You can see them in old parts of San Francisco, including Chinatown, and old parts of downtown Los Angeles. The central district of Coalinga, before the May 1983 earthquake, consisted primarily of such buildings, as do the downtown areas of many cities across the country.

Some of these old buildings contain low-income apartments and are

What was left of the new Stanford University gymnasium (top) and library (bottom) after the April 18, 1906, earthquake can be seen in these photos taken with a box camera the morning of the earthquake by J. B. Wells, a junior at Palo Alto High School. Wells became a professor of structural engineering at Stanford in 1928.

heavily occupied. The costs of strengthening these "disasters waiting to happen" are enormous. Who will pay these costs? The building owners? The public? Where will the occupants live while the work is going on? Will they be able to return, or will the rents go up so that they no longer can afford to live there? Earthquake engineers can handle the technical problems of strengthening these buildings, but society must still resolve the more difficult social and economic problems.

A few communities and private organizations are facing up to the hazards presented by these old structures. The Los Angeles City Council, after ten years of debate, adopted an ordinance in January of 1981 that requires the strengthening of certain old buildings. The ordinance applies to all pre-1934 unreinforced masonry bearing-wall buildings except for detached residential buildings of less than five dwelling units. If alterations on high-occupancy buildings are not completed within three years, they will be demolished. If, however, their walls are anchored within one year, an extension of up to seven years for complete strengthening can be granted. The passage of this ordinance plus the destruction of downtown Coalinga should inspire other cities to adopt similar requirements. San Francisco needs such an ordinance, but in spite of the existence of more than 10,000 old unreinforced masonry buildings within the city, many of which are used as living quarters, there seems little hope for it at the present time. A minimal first step would be to require that a warning notice be posted at the entrance to hazardous structures; people using the buildings then would become aware that unsafe conditions existed and might demand action.

Private owners need not await the passage of new laws before taking action on their own. Two decades ago, Stanford University began a plan of strengthening its old structures on the Quadrangle. At a cost of millions of dollars per year, it has been retrofitting the old sandstone buildings, one by one. After restoration, the exteriors of these buildings appear unchanged, but inside they are supported by new steel and reinforced concrete frames. IBM has been spending large sums of money to protect its buildings and computers in San Jose; the company currently is designing a new computer floor system to resist earthquake shaking.

The People's Republic of China has begun a major program of strengthening old buildings. On a visit to China in 1980 to exchange information on earthquake engineering, we saw several examples of their methods. One scheme consists of placing reinforced concrete beams and columns around the outside of brick buildings, thus enclosing the building in a "cage." At each floor level, tie rods that go completely through the building, from exterior wall to exterior wall, are installed. The ends of these rods are attached to the new beams. This system ties the building together and should prevent collapses such as occurred by the thousands in the 1976

Old brick buildings in China have been strengthened through the addition of a reinforced concrete frame on the outside. The frame is tied to the interior by metal bars. These frames should prevent the total collapses that destroyed Tangshan and killed so many people.

Tangshan earthquake. The possibility of portions of the brick walls falling inward or outward still exists, but such failures would not involve collapse of the building in its entirety. At the time of our visit, the Chinese had upgraded over 70 million square meters (700 million square feet) of building space in this or a similar manner, and the program was continuing.

The value of strengthening buildings was recently demonstrated in Algeria. After the 1954 Orléansville earthquake, the city was rebuilt, many damaged buildings were strengthened, and the city was renamed El Asnam. When another major earthquake struck El Asnam in October 1980, the upgraded buildings performed well, although the city was devastated and many weak structures were destroyed. Efforts are being made to rebuild to higher standards, and the city again has been given a new name, Ech-Cheliff.

The general objective in strengthening existing buildings is to tie the walls, floors, and roof together so that they act as a unit; the building could be compared to a cardboard box that can be knocked about but does not separate into pieces. If a concrete or steel frame is built around the existing building, as in the Chinese method, and if ties are added to hold it together, then collapse of the old structure can be prevented. Such

Bent railroad tracks were left hanging in the air when the hillside fill beneath them slid away during the 1965 Olympia, Washington, earthquake (magnitude 6.6). (Courtesy of University of California, Berkeley)

strengthening can be achieved at a reasonable cost; however, the exterior appearance of the structure is altered. If appearance is an important consideration, then the reinforcement must be built into the interior of the structure and remain invisible, and the cost of strengthening can be extremely high. For historic structures that are to be preserved in their original form, such methods are a necessity.

A less well-recognized but nevertheless serious hazard from old buildings is ornamentation. Many older structures have decorative facades, statuary, and cornices that can break loose and fall to the ground. Parapet walls, marquees, and signs present a similar hazard. Falling debris can block doorways, impede rescue work, and, of course, land on people's heads. Many cities, including San Francisco and Los Angeles, have adopted so-called "parapet ordinances" that require the removal or strengthening of these hazardous building parts. As might be expected, enforcement of such ordinances is difficult because owners do not want to spend the money.

Lifelines

Suppose you have just experienced a major earthquake. The shaking has finally stopped, and you realize that you are unhurt. As you come out from under the table, you hear cries for help from the injured. After providing first aid and making them comfortable, you rush to the telephone to call an ambulance. But the phone is dead, presumably from downed wires. Fortunately, a maintenance man shows up with a two-way radio. He calls for an ambulance, but the response comes that your area is cut off by blocked roads and a damaged overpass. In the meantime, you notice the smell of ·natural gas. When you go to shut off the main gas valve, using the wrench kept handy for that purpose, you become aware that the gas lines have broken in several places and small fires have started. You get a hose and turn on the water, but the flow quickly drops to a trickle because the water mains are broken somewhere and there is no pressure. The final blow comes when you discover the sewage lines are cracked, smelly waste water is seeping onto the street in front of your building, and you are advised not to use the toilets.

This depressing scenario, though exaggerated, has many realistic aspects. The functioning of our daily lives depends heavily upon the operation of society's *lifelines*, which include transportation lines, water supplies, canals, gas lines, power lines, pipelines, and communication links. Their failures in recent earthquakes have drawn attention to their importance, and much research on how to safeguard these facilities is now in progress.

The ability to control fires is essential. Memories of the great San Francisco fire of 1906 still linger in the Bay Area. Water for fighting fires was not available because of broken mains. Later, the city constructed underground water storage tanks at many street intersections, and these supplies are still on standby. Many of the 99,000 deaths in the 1923 Tokyo earthquake were due to the rapidly spreading fires that kept the city ablaze for many days.

Pipelines can be protected by installing flexible joints where the lines cross known faults. Such joints permit large amounts of movement without damage to the lines. Also, automatic shut-off valves can be installed to stop the flow when the pressure drops or when the pipe is subjected to large accelerations. Special gas shut-off devices for the homeowner are now on the market; they react to the shaking of the ground and close the gas valve when the acceleration exceeds a certain limit.

Table 7-2
Community Lifelines

Roads, railways, and bridges for transportation
Transmission lines and generating facilities for electricity
Pipelines and pumping stations for natural gas
Wires, poles, and facilities for telephones and other forms of communication
Pipelines, reservoirs, pumping stations, and canals for water supplies
Pipelines and disposal facilities for sewage and waste water

Toppled equipment at the Sylmar Convertor Station. Dollar losses in equipment exceeded losses in building damage in the 1971 San Fernando earthquake. (Photo by T. L. Youd, courtesy of USGS)

Both the Federal Highway Administration and the California Department of Transportation have established engineering guidelines for protecting existing bridges and overpasses during earthquakes. Many overpasses in California have already undergone retrofitting to prevent them from collapsing during earthquakes, but hundreds more are awaiting attention.

The vulnerability of electrical transmission equipment became apparent during the 1971 San Fernando earthquake. Central switchyards and substations suffered great damage. After considerable development work by the utility companies, in cooperation with university researchers and government agencies, many switchyards were redesigned and retrofitted with earthquake-resistant components. One interesting scheme being tried in California is the installation of *isolators* for critical components, such as circuit breakers and switches. The isolators are rubber pads that separate the equipment from the ground, so that large ground motions are only partially transmitted to the structure. The function of the isolator is similar to that of shock absorbers and springs, which insulate passengers in a vehicle from the roughness of the road.

In established communities, lifelines are already installed and the cost of improving them is formidable; any strengthening or modifications for earthquakes will take many years. In the meantime, however, engineering knowledge of the behavior of lifeline structures is improving, and new installations should be more secure. The margin of safety is also being increased through more advanced operating methods for lifeline systems.

Emergency Facilities

Hospitals, police stations, fire stations, and disaster centers have a crucial role in coping with emergencies. Because these facilities must remain functional during and immediately after an earthquake, more stringent criteria should be applied to their engineering design and construction than to ordinary structures. During the El Asnam earthquake of 1980, the police and fire stations, the hospitals, and the city hall were destroyed. With these facilities gone, emergency help had to be brought in from far-away communities and seriously injured people had to be taken 160 kilometers (almost 100 miles) to Algiers for a well-equipped hospital. Special field hospitals, emergency coordinating centers, and even the city hall offices had to be set up in tents. An unexpected difficulty was caused by the loss of all records, including births, deaths, and marriages, in the collapse of the city hall.

Critical Structures

Certain structures that are particularly dangerous in the event of an earthquake are referred to as *critical structures*: dams, chemical processing plants, oil refineries, liquefied natural gas terminals, and power plants (especially nuclear) are examples. The structures themselves are unusually complicated, and the potential for damage is great in the event of a failure. Designing these facilities to withstand strong ground shaking is a challenge to the engineer.

The seismic design of nuclear power plants involves far more detailed and comprehensive studies than those used for any other buildings. The design process begins with thorough geologic investigations, so that the sources of all possible earthquakes are recognized. The earthquake history of the region is obtained, both from historical records of earthquakes and from on-site field inspections of trenches dug across faults. From this information, the nature of expected earthquake ground motions is determined. Dynamic analyses of the structures and their foundations are made, taking into account the effects of surrounding soils. All pipes and equipment that affect the safe operation of the plant are included in the analyses. With respect to structural design, there is no doubt in our minds that the public is adequately protected against the earthquake hazard.

Dam Safety

Because dams are hazards that affect large numbers of people, they are now inspected regularly by various government agencies to detect any signs of weakness. In the past, however, the seriousness of the earthquake hazard was not fully recognized; several disasters have occurred, notably the near failure of the Lower Van Norman Dam in 1971. Today, more advanced engineering methods and better construction techniques are applied to the design and building of dams. New dams may be considered quite safe against earthquakes, and the threat from old dams has been reduced, where necessary, by strengthening or by limiting the height of the water.

The design of dams is a specialty that involves art as well as science—that is, practical experience plus theoretical knowledge. For instance, in estimating the effects of ground shaking from future earthquakes, judgment and experience must be relied upon because ground motion cannot be predicted precisely. The problems are further complicated by the fact that no two dams are alike—each location differs in its topography, geology, and types of soils and rocks. It is clearly advisable to avoid building a dam in or near active fault zones, although in many regions, such as California, it is impossible to avoid inactive faults because they exist almost everywhere.

The majority of dams are constructed of earth fills, usually clay soils, sands, and gravels. The spaces between the particles of fill material are called pores, and these pores generally contain water. The pore-water pressure must be kept low by adequate drainage of the interior of the dam; if the pressure becomes too high, the fill material loses its strength and the dam may settle or collapse. Increase in pore-water pressure is especially likely to occur during earthquake shaking; that is what happened to the Van Norman dams. Settling of a dam leads to the formation of cracks, and these in turn may permit water to leak through. Once that happens, the dam material begins to wash away, the cracks enlarge, and the dam is torn apart.

Concrete dams are much more expensive than earth-fill dams and therefore not as common. They are usually built in narrow canyons where considerable height is needed (Hoover Dam in Black Canyon on the Colorado River is an example), or on major rivers where an earth dam may not be suitable (for example, Bonneville Dam on the Columbia River). Failure of a concrete dam due to excessive shaking or foundation settlement would be a disaster, but to our knowledge this has never happened.

Once a dam is built, the rate of filling and emptying may have to be controlled to minimize induced seismicity, that is, the creation of earthquakes by the reservoir itself. It may also be desirable to establish zoning controls to restrict the number of people permitted to live in the flood plain of the dam. If the population is kept small, evacuation is easier, and if a failure actually occurs, casualties will be fewer.

One of the largest reservoirs in the San Francisco Bay Area is Crystal Springs Reservoir on the San Francisco peninsula. It is held by Lower Crystal Springs Dam, a concrete gravity dam built in 1890 that survived the 1906 San Francisco earthquake with no apparent damage, even though the San Andreas fault runs through the middle of the reservoir. Since thousands of people live and work in the flood zone of this dam, its safety is crucial. The dam and its rock foundation have been carefully studied in recent years, and the best judgment is that it will be able to withstand another earthquake of magnitude greater than 8.0.

Another dam of great interest to Californians is Auburn Dam on the American River, about 50 kilometers northeast of Sacramento. This dam was originally planned as a concrete arch, 208 meters (685 feet) high and 1,260 meters (4,160 feet) long, which would have made it the largest in the world. Foundation construction began in 1974, at a time when it was assumed that earthquakes were not a hazard in the western foothills of the Sierra Nevada. Then in August 1975 a magnitude 5.9 earthquake occurred near Oroville Dam, about 60 kilometers (35 miles) from the proposed Auburn Dam. The public became alarmed about the safety of the dam, especially since about three-quarters of a million people live in its potential flood plain, and construction was stopped while new geologic studies were made. Almost $100 million had already been spent on preparing the site for the dam when construction was halted. As usually happens when you look for them, earthquake faults were found in the vicinity of the dam. It was decided to change the design of the dam, and both a rock-filled dam and a concrete gravity dam were considered as alternatives to an arch dam. However, it will be many years until new plans are agreed upon, and it is even possible that the dam will be relocated to a different site.

More than 1,000 students and faculty of the Tangshan Institute of Mining and Metallurgy were killed in the 1976 earthquake. Survivors erected the temporary classrooms (background) so that classes could continue. The destroyed library is in the foreground.

The Greatest Earthquake Disaster of Modern Times

On the morning of July 28, 1976, at 3:42 A.M. local time, a magnitude 7.8 earthquake occurred directly under Tangshan, China, a city of about a million people located 160 kilometers (100 miles) due east of Beijing. The entire city was leveled and 240,000 people were killed. The damaged facilities included not only buildings but collapsed bridges, bent railroad tracks, overturned trains, damaged highways, toppled chimneys, broken pipes, and cracked dams. The economic loss was about 3 billion yuan (or $2 billion).

The earthquake was felt for at least 800 kilometers (500 miles) in all directions. In Tianjin, the provincial capital about 110 kilometers southwest of Tangshan, as well as in Beijing and many other cities, millions of people immediately evacuated their buildings and moved outdoors to be safe from the effects of aftershocks. American tourists who were moved out of their hotels in Beijing reported that the Chinese were well prepared for evacuation and that everyone moved quietly and promptly.

A major aftershock occurred at 6:45 P.M. the same day. It had a magnitude of 7.1 and was centered only a few kilometers from the main early morning earthquake. In Tangshan this second earthquake destroyed what little had survived the first one. The losses were so huge because almost none of the structures in Tangshan were designed to

The survivors of the Tangshan earthquake built huts from the rubble. Several hundred thousand people were housed in such quarters until the rebuilding of the city could be completed.

resist seismic forces. The most common type of construction used un-reinforced brick walls, which quickly fell down during the shaking.

All four of the city's hospitals were destroyed and the seriously injured had to be taken to other cities. The army built temporary shelters for medical workers and injured people. The entire city was sprayed with disinfectant chemicals from helicopters and planes to control the spread of disease. Fear of an epidemic was justified because it took a long time to remove the thousands of bodies from under the rubble.

Transportation by air soon became available, but all railways were damaged and unusable for some time. Water supply was a serious problem because most pipelines were broken—one survivor told us that it was two days before he could get water. Diesel engines were set up to pump water from wells until the pipelines could be repaired, and military trucks were used to distribute drinking water for about 10 days. Trucks brought water all the way from Beijing and Tianjin. Very few fires followed the earthquake, primarily because the construction was mostly of brick and there were no gas lines in the city.

Today, Tangshan is largely rebuilt under a new city plan and a new seismic building code. The rebuilding of Tangshan was one of the world's greatest construction projects, involving not only new apartments for a million people but also new roads, bridges, sewer lines, factories, power plants, schools, stores, and every other facility needed for a major city.

This view looking south from Daly City shows the San Andreas fault running through San Andreas lake (A) and entering the Pacific Ocean at the landslide area (B). A school (C) is situated directly on the fault. Several homes located at the edge of the landslide were undermined and have been removed since this picture was taken. Today, this type of development directly on the fault would probably not be permitted. (Photo by R. E. Wallace, courtesy of USGS)

8

Community and Individual Planning

There was a heavy grinding noise as of brick houses rubbing together. . . . As I reeled about on the pavement trying to keep my footing, I saw a sight! The entire front of a tall four-story brick building in Third Street sprung outward like a door and fell sprawling across the street.
—Mark Twain, *Roughing It*

NO ONE CAN TELL YOU precisely how to plan and prepare for earthquakes, but if you understand them, you will be in a position to make intelligent decisions. Most people who are making plans ask questions like these: Will there be another great earthquake? What will happen to my community? Should I do anything about my property? They also inquire about zoning restrictions, government disaster relief, and earthquake insurance. These matters are discussed in this chapter; individual preparedness is discussed in the next chapter.

Will There Be Another Great Earthquake?

This is the question we are most frequently asked by Californians. The answer, of course, is "yes," because great earthquakes are inevitable in California, as Mark Twain found out as he strolled down Third Street in San Francisco in 1865. Many years have elapsed since the last large earthquakes on the San Andreas fault (they occurred in 1906 in northern California and 1857 in southern California). In the intervening years, the fault has remained "locked"—that is, no significant strain release has occurred. Nevertheless, the North American and Pacific plates have continued to slide inexorably past each other at a rate of about 6 centimeters (2.5 inches) per year, which means that large strains have accumulated in the rocks

Stores along University Avenue in Palo Alto after the 1906 earthquake. (Photo by W. C. Mendenhall, courtesy of USGS)

and a potential for several meters (10 to 20 feet) of fault slip now exists.

Reliable scientific estimates place the probability of a great earthquake (magnitude 7.5 or greater) in California at approximately 50 percent within the next 30 years. Southern California is a more likely site for the next great earthquake than northern California, because the interval since its last large earthquake is about 50 years longer. Such probabilistic estimates are not predictions; they do not tell us when the next earthquake will come or where it will take place. What they do tell us is that millions of people now living in California will become victims of a large earthquake and should be planning accordingly.

Great earthquakes in the U.S. are not limited to the San Andreas fault. The "noble earthquake" described by John Muir (p. 83) occurred in the Owens Valley, east of the Sierra Nevada, and its magnitude is estimated as 8.5. Others have occurred during the past 175 years in Nevada, Alaska, Hawaii, and the central Mississippi River valley. While it is theoretically possible to have a great earthquake in any state at any time, in most places the probabilities are so low that they cannot be taken seriously for everyday purposes. Moderate-size earthquakes (magnitude 5.5 to 7.5) have taken place in Idaho, Montana, New York, South Carolina, Texas, Utah, Washington, and Wyoming, and smaller earthquakes occur occasionally in almost every state. On the average, about 400 earthquakes large enough to cause building damage (even though minor damage) occur in the conterminous U.S. every year.

What Will Happen to My Home and Community?

Planning agencies at all levels of government attempt to answer this question by means of engineering studies and detailed observations of the effects of earthquakes in other communities. Studies of earthquake losses during simulated earthquakes have been conducted for the Los Angeles region and the San Francisco Bay region; the results are summarized in Table 1-1, p. 8. The staggering figures for deaths, injuries, and damage emphasize the need for sound planning to reduce the expected losses.

Damage to single-family homes may range from only a few cracks in the walls to shifting and tilting of the entire building. Broken windows, bent door frames with jammed doors, cracked masonry walls, and cracked foundations are common. Chimneys often crack apart or pull away from the house; this can be prevented if the chimney is reinforced with steel bars and fastened by metal straps to the frame of the house. An old house may not be properly attached to the foundations by anchor bolts, with the result that it can shift off the foundation during an earthquake. To repair the resulting damage, which usually includes broken water, gas, and sewer pipes, is very costly. Newer houses are usually properly anchored, but to find out for certain, you must crawl under the house and inspect the base plates at the bottom of the exterior walls. If the house is anchored, the heads of the bolts will be visible, usually 4 to 6 feet apart.

Houses located on hillsides in fault zones may be totally lost during earthquakes, especially if the ground is saturated from rainfall. Preventive measures are extremely expensive and there is no guarantee that they will be able to stop the side of a hill from moving. In flat, low-lying areas, especially near bodies of water, the danger comes from liquefaction and settlement of the ground; again, the damage can range from minor cracking to a total loss. Of course, a house located directly on a fault line, where the rupture can crack the surface of the earth, may also be totally lost.

In spite of these possibilities for damage to dwellings, it is still true that a single-family house of wood-frame construction is a relatively safe structure. These buildings can deform and shift extensively without collapsing, and serious injuries to the occupants are rare. This fact was borne out in the Coalinga earthquake of May 1983, in which several hundred homes were badly damaged. We inspected some that were thrown off their foundations and tilted dramatically; the occupants were given a wild

In the 1983 Coalinga, California, earthquake, the roofs and walls of many old brick and masonry buildings collapsed.

ride (like a "bucking bronco," one said) but escaped with only abrasions and bruises. Falling objects, toppling furniture, and moving refrigerators are the most common hazards to people in wood-frame houses.

In a typical community, the greatest building damage during an earthquake is the collapse of old buildings constructed of poor quality masonry with little or no reinforcement. In Coalinga, for example, most of the buildings in the downtown shopping area were of this type. The walls and roofs collapsed, leaving the interiors and the sidewalks piled with bricks and rubble. Rebuilding a community takes years, and in the meantime people suffer from economic loss and unemployment. The only remedy is to strengthen or replace these buildings in advance, and a few communities are attempting to do so. Such efforts are worthwhile because it has been amply demonstrated that properly constructed buildings can survive earthquakes with only minor damage. For example, we inspected a relatively new reinforced concrete building in downtown Coalinga that had barely a crack in it, while old masonry buildings adjacent to it on two sides had been reduced to rubble.

Should I Do Anything About My Property?

All building owners should become familiar with the geological hazards that may affect their property. One obvious consideration is the location

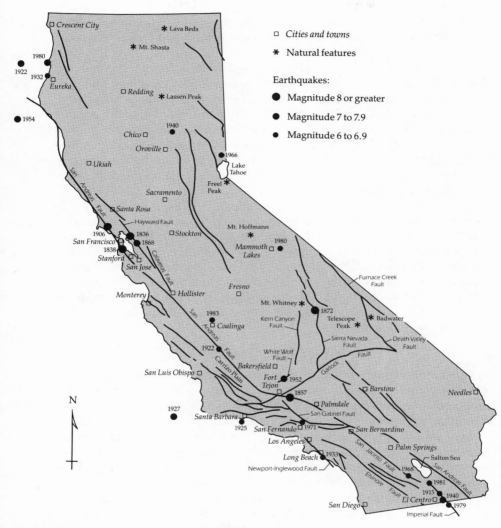

Figure 8-1. Major faults and earthquakes of California.

of the building with respect to faults, especially active ones. Such faults are the primary hazards, but even inactive ones can rupture and surprise everyone (the fault that created the Coalinga earthquake is in this category).

Other hazards, including landslides and liquefaction, should also be identified. The United States Geological Survey (USGS) and the California Division of Mines and Geology (CDMG) have prepared maps identifying the regions susceptible to these hazards. If you are located in such a region, the remedial measures include strengthening of the building, installation of retaining walls, injection of grout into unstable soils, and drainage of water. If you contemplate such action, you should begin by consulting a structural engineer, geotechnical engineer, or geologist, depending upon the nature of the problem.

Strengthening of a structure can sometimes be done inexpensively; for example, frames can be bolted to foundations, braces can be added between posts and beams, and chimneys can be tied to the frame. However, the removal of walls and ceilings to install bracing is an expensive undertaking. Extensive alterations of this kind were made on the State Capitol Building in Sacramento and on the Stanford Quadrangle. If you wish to determine the present condition of a building and the feasible methods of strengthening it, you should consult a structural engineer who is familiar with this type of work.

Zoning and Land-Use Planning

It is easy to recognize the need for proper controls on the use of land in seismic regions, but it is difficult to enact suitable legislation. Whenever an agency of government tells a landowner what he can or cannot do with his property, controversy is likely to arise. Every city council and planning commission knows the difficulties of trying to resolve the classic conflict between the rights of the individual and the rights of the community. In seismic areas the difficult questions are these: What limitations should be placed on construction in areas near active faults, or where the soil is poor, or where landslides may occur, or that are liquefaction-prone, or that might be flooded by a dam failure? If indiscriminate building is allowed in such areas, the likelihood of property damage and loss of life from earthquakes is increased, thus creating a burden for the rest of the community.

The zoning process begins with geological studies of the hazards. Maps are prepared showing the earthquake faults and the epicenters of past earthquakes. Further studies identify potential landslide areas, liquefaction-prone areas, regions where the ground is likely to settle, areas that might flood if a dam were to fail, and coastal areas where tsunamis could cause damage. All such information is printed on maps that are available to the public from the U.S. Geological Survey and from county governments.

With the aid of this information, planning agencies must decide what restrictions to place on building in the hazardous areas. The most extreme action is to ban all construction, although the area may still be quite suitable for recreational purposes—parks, campgrounds, and hiking trails offer little or no risk. In other cases, limitations on building, rather than a total ban, may be appropriate. For instance, hospitals, schools, and other important structures can be ruled out; also, limitations can be placed on the type of construction and the heights of buildings. Furthermore, the buildings that are permitted in a hazardous area can be required to meet higher engineering requirements as compared to the same buildings located elsewhere.

Disaster Relief

Earthquake damage in the United States up to now has been relatively small compared to that caused by floods, hurricanes, and tornadoes, but this situation is likely to be reversed. Because of the growth of population, especially on the West Coast, the potential for damage and life loss from an earthquake is now greater than that from any other hazard. To provide assistance after a major disaster, the U.S. Congress passed the Federal Disaster Relief Act in 1974. This law provides for the repair and restoration of publicly owned facilities and assistance to individuals in the form of temporary housing, low interest loans, and grants. First priority is given

A shopping center in San Fernando suffered such severe damage that it was razed after the 1971 earthquake. (Photo by R. E. Wallace, courtesy of USGS)

Earthquake Rescue and Relief
El Asnam, Algeria

Researchers at the John A. Blume Earthquake Engineering Center, Stanford University, under the direction of Professor H. C. Shah, have worked with the Algerian government on earthquake-related problems since 1976. In 1978 the Stanford researchers made a seismic hazard analysis of Algeria that identified the El Asnam region as having the highest probability for the next large earthquake. Then, on October 10, 1980, at approximately 1:30 P.M., El Asnam was struck by an earthquake of magnitude 7.3. The next day a request for technical assistance was transmitted to Stanford by the government of Algeria. Shah and two graduate students left immediately for Algeria and reached Algiers the next morning. Their mission was to help the Algerian government in assessing damage to buildings and other facilities.

During the hours following the earthquake, the government of El Asnam began organizing rescue and relief operations. However, the disaster was so immense that local authorities could not handle it on their own, and about 24 hours after the earthquake, the district of El Asnam was put under military rule. Armed personnel patrolled the city to prevent looting. All traffic, even emergency vehicles, had to pass through military check points. Only medical and rescue units, military personnel, and government advisors were allowed to enter the city. The 125,000 survivors were evacuated from El Asnam to special tent cities set up by the army about 5 kilometers away.

Rescue of people buried in the rubble but still alive continued for several days. Special dogs, trained in Switzerland for avalanche rescue work and capable of distinguishing between live and dead bodies buried under the debris, were brought in to locate survivors. Corpses were sprayed with a transparent plastic liquid that hardened immediately, allowing identification of bodies but controlling disease and odor. Survivors were inoculated against cholera and typhoid.

Even as rescue work was continuing, the engineering teams examined the condition of buildings that were still standing. Those that had to be torn down by the military demolition crews were marked with red paint. Buildings that were safe for occupancy were marked in green, and those that required further evaluation were marked in orange.

After one week, water and electricity were again available and rail and road transportation to and from El Asnam was resumed. In two weeks, the emergency situation was over. All bodies had been recovered, and the seriously injured had been transferred to hospitals as far away as Algiers (160 kilometers east of El Asnam). More than 2,000 people died, and about 20,000 were injured.

Today, most of the population is living in prefabricated houses. The city of El Asnam, once called Orléansville, has been renamed Ech-Cheliff. With many of its buildings destroyed and its social structure and economy disrupted, the challenge of rebuilding El Asnam into a seismically resistant and economically healthy Ech-Cheliff still remains.

Recovering bodies from the rubble of collapsed buildings in El Asnam was slow and discouraging work. The odor of decomposing bodies was overpowering; a piece of cloth saturated with eucalyptus oil helped overcome the smell.

The control tower at the Anchorage International Airport, about 75 miles from the epicenter, collapsed during the 1964 earthquake. One person was killed and another injured. (Photo by the Federal Aviation Agency, courtesy of USGS)

to rebuilding public property; assistance to individuals is provided only if funds are still available. The conditions for federal aid are carefully circumscribed, and funds can be authorized only by a Presidential Declaration. The adequacy of this legislation as it applies to large-scale, long-range reconstruction remains to be seen. At the present time, communities are uncertain about the nature and extent of federal support they can expect. The act was also intended to encourage loss-reduction measures through sound land-use planning and construction regulations. Other forms of federal aid to individuals include food stamps and income tax deductions.

The Earthquake Hazards Reduction Act of 1977 was an attempt to reduce the risks to life and property from earthquakes. The federal government designated the Federal Emergency Management Agency (FEMA) as the primary agency in charge of all pre- and post-earthquake federal assistance. This act relies heavily on a partnership between federal, state, county, and city governments to accomplish its goals. Since passage of the law, the federal government has provided active leadership in all of the following activities:

- Disaster planning and emergency response procedures
- Earthquake prediction
- Seismic risk assessments
- Codes and construction standards
- Reduction of hazards from existing buildings and facilities
- Safety of critical facilities
- Public education programs
- Studies of earthquakes and their effects through cooperative international programs

Because we have not had a major earthquake since these two laws were passed, their value in reducing losses has not yet been assessed.

Earthquake Insurance

In view of the uncertainty surrounding public financial assistance to individuals after an earthquake, it is prudent to consider providing your own protection through insurance. Earthquake insurance first became available in California about ten years after the 1906 San Francisco earthquake. For many years, in spite of low rates (about 40¢ per $1,000 coverage with a 5 percent deductible), very few people purchased insurance. Possible reasons are the misconception that other types of insurance would cover earthquake-related losses and the fact that the insurance companies made little effort to promote earthquake insurance. By the time of the 1925 Santa Barbara earthquake, only a small number of earthquake policies had been written and therefore the insurance companies had few claims to pay. After the 1971 San Fernando earthquake (which caused almost $500 million in damage), only about $12 million in claims were submitted and about 23 percent of this amount was actually paid. The number of earthquake policies has increased since then, although less than 5 percent of California homeowners had purchased earthquake insurance by 1975. Most earthquake insurance is on commercial and industrial property, not on residential property.

Earthquake insurance is available from most of the companies that provide owners and tenants with conventional insurance against fire, theft, and other such perils. Coverage usually includes damage to buildings, mobile homes, contents, and personal belongings, if caused directly by an earthquake. Fire damage resulting from an earthquake is usually covered by standard fire insurance policies.

Because they are intended to insure against catastrophes rather than against small losses, earthquake insurance policies usually have a deductible amount that is either a percent of the insured value or a fixed dollar amount. For homeowners and tenants insurance, the deductible is often 5 percent of the insured value, applied separately to the building

The 1933 Long Beach earthquake (magnitude 6.3) threw this house off its foundation walls. This type of damage can be prevented by bolting the house to the foundation, an important measure in strengthening older homes. (Courtesy of USGS)

and to its contents. Under this plan, if a home is insured for $100,000 on the building and $50,000 on the contents, the homeowner pays for earthquake damage up to $5,000 on the building and $2,500 on the contents. The insurance covers the remainder of the losses, up to the maximum insured value. Most companies require that the coverage equal the full value of the house, just as with fire insurance.

The cost of earthquake insurance depends primarily upon location, type of construction, and soil conditions. California is presently divided into insurance zones, each of which is assigned a rate level according to the probability and severity of expected earthquakes. The lowest rates are in the central part of the state, the next higher rates are along part of the coast and in the Sierra Nevada, the next higher rates are along the San Andreas fault, and the highest rates are in Imperial County in southern California. From the standpoint of construction, the lowest rates apply to small wood-frame houses. The rates increase progressively for buildings made with steel frames, reinforced concrete, masonry veneer or masonry walls, reinforced masonry, and unreinforced masonry. Special soil or geological conditions can mean higher rates; for example, a building on filled land might be subject to a 25 percent surcharge. Of course, many poorly constructed or hazardously located buildings are uninsurable.

A typical annual premium for earthquake coverage for a small wood-frame house located in the coastal zone of California and not on filled land is $1.50 per $1,000 of coverage, with a 5 percent deductible. In higher risk locations, the premium for such a house might be as much as $4.00 per $1,000 of coverage. For buildings with very high risks, the premiums can go as high as $50 per $1,000 of coverage.

It is surprising that so little earthquake insurance coverage exists in most communities. Consider Los Angeles and Orange Counties, which are located between the San Andreas fault and the Newport-Inglewood fault, both of which are active and produce large earthquakes. The potential loss in these counties from a single major earthquake is estimated at $90 billion, but only $1 billion of earthquake insurance coverage is in effect.

Why is it that so many companies and individuals have not purchased earthquake insurance? One obvious reason is that insurance companies do not actively promote such insurance, presumably because of the burden that huge numbers of claims following a major earthquake would place upon them. A few insurance companies even refuse to provide earthquake coverage. Another reason is that banks and lending agencies, even in highly seismic California, do not require mortgagees to have earthquake insurance (although they do require fire insurance). Also, people probably assume that they can rely on federal or state disaster aid after a major earthquake. While financial aid may indeed be available, it must be remembered that it is primarily in the form of loans, not gifts. After the 1971 San Fernando earthquake (magnitude 6.6) the federal government provided over $250 million in low-interest loans, but many who applied were turned down. After a much larger earthquake, say magnitude 8.0, the losses might be a hundred times what they were in 1971. It is unlikely that federal funds could accommodate the resulting demand for loans and other forms of aid.

Table 8-1

Earthquake Insurance

Example 1 (Fully insured house)
Replacement value of house = $100,000
Amount of insurance = $100,000 with 5% deductible
Annual premium = $1.50 per $1,000 of insurance, or $150

Percent Damage to House During Earthquake	5%	15%	25%	100%
Amount of damage	$5,000	$15,000	$25,000	$100,000
Damage covered by insurance (100%)	$5,000	$15,000	$25,000	$100,000
Deductible	$5,000	$5,000	$5,000	$5,000
Paid by insurance	0	$10,000	$20,000	$95,000
Paid by owner	$5,000	$5,000	$5,000	$5,000

Cumulative Value of $150 Per Year Premium			
Annual rate of interest	After 10 years	After 20 years	After 30 years
0	$1,500	$3,000	$4,500
6%	$2,100	$5,850	$12,600
12%	$2,950	$12,100	$40,500

How to use the data:
Assume that the house is expected to suffer 25% damage in the next 30 years. Also, assume 6% interest over a 30-year period. Then the insurance will pay back more than the value of the premiums ($20,000 versus $12,600). However, if only 5% damage is expected, the insurance will pay back nothing.

By making your own estimates of expected damage and by considering your own financial condition, you can judge whether earthquake insurance is a desirable option for you.

Example 2 (Partially insured house)
Replacement value of house = $100,000
Amount of insurance = $80,000 with 5% deductible
Annual premium = $1.50 per $1,000 of insurance, or $120

Percent Damage to House During Earthquake	5%	15%	25%	100%
Amount of damage	$5,000	$15,000	$25,000	$100,000
Damage covered by insurance (80%)	$4,000	$12,000	$20,000	$80,000
Deductible	$4,000	$4,000	$4,000	$4,000
Paid by insurance	0	$8,000	$16,000	$76,000
Paid by owner	$5,000	$7,000	$9,000	$24,000

Cumulative Value of $120 Per Year Premium			
Annual rate of interest	After 10 years	After 20 years	After 30 years
0	$1,200	$2,400	$3,600
6%	$1,680	$4,680	$10,100
12%	$2,360	$9,680	$32,400

The typical 5 percent deductible on homeowners earthquake insurance policies presents another deterrent to the purchase of insurance. Because modern wood-frame houses usually suffer only moderate damage in earthquakes, the chances that the loss will exceed the deductible are not great. For the 12,000 homes in the region of strong ground shaking during the 1971 San Fernando earthquake, the average cost of repairs was about 6.6 percent of total value. About 3,000 homes sustained damage of over 5 percent, but only a few houses suffered 100 percent damage and had to be replaced. The remainder had damages amounting to less than 5 percent. On the basis of these figures, some people argue that money is more wisely spent on strengthening buildings than on insurance premiums.

If you are thinking of buying insurance, here are some of the factors you should consider:

- Proximity to active earthquake faults
- Seismic history of the region (frequency of occurrence of earthquakes; time since last earthquake)
- Building construction (type of building and foundation; architectural layout; materials used; quality of workmanship; extent to which earthquake resistance was considered by the designer)
- Local site conditions (type and condition of soil; slope of the land; fill material; geologic structure of the earth beneath; annual rainfall)
- Value of the building and its contents
- Cost of the insurance and restrictions on coverage
- Your financial condition and emotional attitude

Statistical and engineering methods are available that make it possible to perform risk-benefit calculations based upon the preceding factors. Such calculations can help in arriving at an insurance decision, but they require detailed and technical consideration of each specific building and its location.

Stanford University recently made a careful study of its buildings and the hazards presented by the nearby San Andreas and Hayward faults. The conclusion was that a major earthquake could produce up to 10 percent damage on a campus-wide basis. The replacement cost of all campus buildings and their contents is about $1.4 billion; this figure includes not only the main academic areas but also the Stanford University Medical Center and the Stanford Shopping Center. The university purchased earthquake insurance in the amount of $125 million on buildings and contents (about 9 percent of the total value), with a deductible equal to 3 percent of the damage, but not less than $3 million.

Because the university has scores of buildings, calculations can be based on average amounts of damage, recognizing that the damage to any one

Typical damage to mobile homes. This home was knocked off its support piers during the 1979 Imperial Valley earthquake. (Courtesy of *California Geology*)

building may be very high and that to another building may be very low. For individual homeowners, knowing that the damage ratio in the community may be 10 percent is not very helpful, because your home may be the one to receive 100 percent damage. As a result, each homeowner usually must insure for full value. It would be interesting to explore the possibility of an insurance policy for an entire community, say for 10 percent of the total value, with each homeowner contributing to the premium.

Our personal insurance decisions were as follows: One of the authors purchased earthquake coverage for his house many years ago and has continued it ever since, believing that it becomes more valuable each year. The other purchased insurance in 1981, after comparing the annualized expected losses with the annual premiums. Incidentally, both houses are located about four miles from the San Andreas fault. Naturally, many personal factors entered into these decisions. For instance, our professional work has made us earthquake conscious and, being engineers, we are inclined to take protective measures. (Also, as you might expect, our homes are our biggest investments; it would be a financial disaster if we lost them.)

A few months ago, a new development in earthquake insurance occurred—one company advertised widely the availability of a new form of homeowners earthquake insurance. This insurance has no deductible amount, and coverage does not have to be at full value of the house. A typical annual premium is $50 for $25,000 coverage. The advertisements pointed out that this insurance could be used to cover the deductible amount on a standard homeowners insurance policy. It is reported that the new policies are popular and that the number of policies sold far exceeds expectations.

When school resumed in Coalinga, California, after the May 1983 earthquake, this first-grade class brushed up on what to do during the next one: Get under the desk, face away from the window, and cover your head. (Courtesy of Wide World Photos)

9

Preparing for the Next Earthquake

Earthquakes don't kill people, buildings do.
                    —Earthquake engineers' maxim

THOSE OF US who live in earthquake regions must accept the fact that a major earthquake may occur at any moment. This realization does not deter us from going about our daily activities at work, school, home, and other places. We accept the risks from earthquakes just as we accept the risks from vehicles on highways and streets. However, we can greatly lower the risks by preparing for earthquakes and knowing what to do when they come.

All earthquake preparedness efforts—whether by individuals, small businesses, large industrial companies, utilities, or government agencies—are aimed at reducing the number of injuries and deaths, reducing the amount of damage to property and records, and hastening the process of recovery. These aims can be achieved by making preparations in the following three categories:

- Reduction of the risk (before the earthquake)
- Emergency response (when the earthquake comes)
- Restoration of facilities and service (after the earthquake)

Some preparations can be made by individuals acting alone; others require governmental action and the expenditures of large sums of money.

Reduction of the risk. The first step in reducing losses is to identify the risks; for instance, structures and premises can be inspected to identify weaknesses and unsafe conditions. The next step is to take corrective action; for example, buildings can be strengthened, and equipment and contents can be braced or tied down.

Emergency response. Coping with a disaster is the responsibility of everyone. Experience has shown that most people begin immediately to help others and to take steps to reduce further damage. They assist those in charge and generally "pitch in" as needed. Because many important decisions must be made on the spot by volunteers, it helps if they have had prior training.

In any disaster we depend primarily upon police, fire, and medical personnel. They rehearse and prepare for a variety of disasters, and they have access to communications, transportation, and emergency supplies (including radios, generators, tools, flashlights, breathing equipment, and medical supplies). The work that must be done includes providing medical assistance, searching for those who are trapped within buildings, controlling fires and chemical spills, evacuating people, handling communications, shutting down facilities, preventing looting, and dealing with other problems that arise. After the immediate emergency is over, it is essential to provide safe drinking water, food, sanitary facilities, and emergency housing. The next tasks are to organize clean-up and repair work, control access to damaged buildings, prepare photographic documentation of the damage, protect vital records, make engineering studies, etc.

Restoration of facilities and services. Recovery consists of a gradual restoration of normal activities; for instance, facilities must be repaired, production and business resumed, and people rehabilitated. The task may be monumental, but it will be easier if plans for restoration have been developed ahead of time.

The amount of effort that goes into earthquake preparedness depends upon the available resources, the extent of the potential losses, and community and management commitment. Stanford University, for example, has formed an Earthquake Action Group, composed of key administrative and safety personnel, that meets regularly to review plans for coping with the next earthquake. Among many other projects, the group sponsors training and educational programs for staff and students.

Contents of Buildings

Building owners, businesses, and utilities are now taking steps to protect their investments in equipment, furniture, machinery, and products—and with good reason. In the 1978 Santa Barbara and 1979 San Fernando earthquakes the dollar loss in equipment and contents was far greater than the loss in damage to buildings. This situation is likely to be repeated, especially as more businesses install computers and other electronic equipment. Imagine the consequences of losing computer hardware and software; how would banks, businesses, and governments operate?

Even during moderate earthquakes equipment and contents of buildings are major hazards to people. In offices, for example, unbraced bookcases,

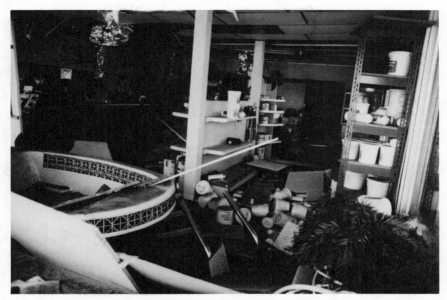

Interior of a store in Coalinga, California, after the 1983 earthquake (magnitude 6.5).

file cabinets, and storage cabinets can tip over. In shops, machinery can fall or slide into people. In laboratories, bottles and other containers commonly fall from shelves and break on floors and countertops. Compressed gas cylinders fall over if not properly restrained. Dangerous liquids in tanks may slosh and spill over. In gymnasiums, banks of lockers can fall over. In classrooms and auditoriums, ceiling tiles, light fixtures, and overhead equipment can break loose and fall onto the seats. In museums, valuable objects can be broken or damaged by falling from shelves or hooks. In living areas, heavy stereo equipment can slide from shelves. In kitchens, refrigerators and stoves may slide across the floor and slam into someone. The list of such hazards goes on and on; you can add to it simply by scrutinizing your surroundings.

To protect against these hazards, some relatively simple and inexpensive measures can be taken. Computers can be bolted to floors and braced to ceilings; sensitive electronic equipment can be padded. Furniture and equipment can be attached to the walls by screws and metal clips. Machinery can be braced by metal straps and securely bolted to floors. Bottles on shelves can be protected by installing lips along the front edges of the shelves or by using elastic shock cords. Compressed gas cylinders can be attached to wall supports by strong cables or chains. Tanks containing liquids can be well braced and their lids can be made secure. Lockers can be braced by strips of wood attached to their tops and to the walls. Lighting

If not anchored adequately, storage cylinders and tanks can be hazardous during an earthquake. These cylinders fell over during the 1983 Coalinga earthquake.

fixtures can be braced and mounted securely. Overhead equipment can be securely attached to beams and columns. Art objects can be held by fine wires or strings. Heavy or expensive equipment can be removed from upper shelves and stored on lower ones. Remedies such as these are not difficult to carry out, yet they provide large benefits by reducing both material losses and injuries.

Sometimes people make the mistake of testing the seismic safety of objects by their "feel"—they push against a heavy refrigerator, for example, and conclude that it is not going to move or tip because of its large mass. This is, of course, a fallacy. During an earthquake the effective force that moves or topples an object actually comes from the inertia of the object itself, and this inertial force is directly proportional to the mass. Thus, an object weighing 500 pounds is just as likely to fall over during an earthquake as an object weighing 50 pounds, if they are the same size and if their centers of gravity are in the same location. However, the heavier object will certainly produce more serious injury.

Educational Programs

Everyone living, working, or traveling in a seismic region should be knowledgeable about earthquakes; you can learn from reading, from television, from lectures and slide shows, and from talking to others. Programs on seismic safety should be presented regularly to students and teachers, company employees, government workers, and other groups. Building managers and persons responsible for safety in buildings should be properly trained in the elements of seismic safety.

School children should be given basic instruction in the causes of earthquakes, what they feel like, and how to prepare for them. Merely knowing the facts about earthquakes can help greatly to reduce anxiety and provide reassurance for children. They should be taught the rudiments of plate tectonics in order to dispel any wild notions about California falling into the sea or the earth opening up and swallowing people.

Every school should conduct earthquake drills so that pupils can learn what to do if an earthquake occurs during school hours. Families of school children should make plans for getting together after an earthquake; this may help to avoid "parent panic" and the resulting frantic phone calls that overload the phone system and interfere with essential work.

Earthquake Drills

Earthquake drills are remarkably effective in testing preparedness plans and pinpointing deficiencies. A recent earthquake drill at Stanford University included hospital personnel, the police and fire departments, facilities personnel, and students. The scenario specified a magnitude 7.5 earthquake with its epicenter on the San Andreas fault about 30 kilometers (20 miles) away. On the basis of this information, the number of casualties and the extent of building damage was estimated. Broken water and sewer lines, fires, chemical spills, blocked roads, and dozens of other problems and hazards were also specified in the scenario. Mock casualties at a residence hall and a classroom building tested the medical personnel (the casualties were assigned realistic injuries and made up to look the part). Campus workers, hospital personnel, police and fire personnel, and administrators who participated in the drill had no advance knowledge of the precise problems they would be expected to cope with. Instead, they were presented spontaneously with a variety of crises during the minutes and hours immediately following the imaginary earthquake. Scores of unforeseen problems arose, including breakdowns in communications, inability to care for the large numbers of casualties, inadequate supplies, and difficulties in allocating manpower. The drill aroused the public to the great need for earthquake preparedness, and many corrective steps were soon initiated.

The value of such educational efforts was apparent after the 1979 earthquake in southern California. A post-earthquake study of the behavior of the 123 people who were working in the Imperial County Services Building at the time of the earthquake showed some interesting patterns. Seventy percent of the occupants said that their first action was based upon previous instructions in classes or drills. Almost everyone got under a desk, stood in a doorway, or stayed put. There was no panic, although the building shook violently and nearly collapsed (it was later demolished). There were numerous minor injuries, such as bruises and bumps, but no one was seriously hurt. Here is the experience of one worker on the second floor of the building:

> At the time of the earthquake, I was convinced that the building was going to collapse and that I was going to die. Because of this feeling I felt it was necessary to get under my desk. Then the shaking increased; I could no longer stand up and crawled under my desk. After the shaking stopped, I wondered if I could get down the stairway without being trampled to death. When I got out, I crossed the street, was counted, and told to go home. I had no concept of time and was in a state of shock. I started walking home (I live 12 or 13 miles from work) and was found by my husband.*

Psychological Reactions to Earthquakes

Because most people have never experienced a major disaster and are not trained to cope with one, they may suffer emotional stress and behave irrationally. Such behavior can be avoided, or at least reduced, by proper education and training. The disciplined behavior of police, fire, military, and Red Cross personnel demonstrates the effectiveness of their training.

Even trained people may experience a short period of confusion after a damaging earthquake. A little time is needed to realize what has happened, to take stock of the situation, and to decide what to do first. Some people will begin immediately to help others, while others may remain stunned for quite some time. One abnormal reaction is to become totally immobilized; people in this condition are numbed to the destruction around them and act as if they were alone in the world. They do not respond to the needs of the situation and are unable to help themselves. The opposite reaction is to become overactive and fuss about in a flurry of helter-skelter, useless activity, perhaps even interfering with necessary rescue work. Extreme stress may produce perspiration, rapid breathing, nausea, and weakness of the muscles in anyone; however, most normal people, if unhurt, will regain their composure in a very short time.

One of the dangers, especially in crowded areas, is that someone will panic and behave wildly. A person in panic loses all sense of judgment and behaves in a senseless manner, sometimes imparting terror to others. The danger, of course, is that the entire crowd will be thrown into panic. In 1976, immediately after the great Guatemalan earthquake (magnitude

---

* Quoted in Arnold, C., Eisner, R., Durkin, M., and Whitaker, D., "Imperial County Services Building: Occupant Behavior and Operational Consequences as a Result of the 1979 Imperial Valley Earthquake," August 1982, Building Systems Development, Inc., San Mateo, California.

7.5), one of the authors (Haresh Shah) went to Guatemala City to work with Guatemalan earthquake engineers. While he was lecturing about recovery plans to a large group of people in an auditorium, a major aftershock occurred. The first reaction of the audience was to panic and run for the exits. With the building still creaking and shaking, it was difficult to maintain order; fortunately, the pleas of the speaker were heeded, and a stampede was avoided.

Among the serious long-term effects of a strong earthquake on both children and adults is psychological damage. The loss of a sense of security and the feeling of helplessness can be overwhelming. Each new aftershock adds to the emotional strains and brings forth the same terrifying questions: What is going to be destroyed next? Will I survive this one? It is essential for parents to remain calm during such a stressful time—shrieking adults greatly upset children and add to their already serious anxieties.

The 1971 San Fernando earthquake occurred at 6:10 A.M., when most people were in bed. Home, bedroom, and especially bed represent security to a child, and that security was destroyed by the earthquake. The darkness of the hour added to the children's fears. In a number of homes that suffered only minor structural damage, an unexpected problem occurred:

Earthquake preparations are taken seriously in Japan, where the government spends large sums of money on education and preventive measures. This "typical" room is mounted on a truck equipped with a shaking device that simulates an earthquake for the "residents." (Photo by H. Krawinkler, Stanford University)

the doors jammed. Bedroom door frames became warped, the doors wouldn't open, and frightened children were isolated from their parents.

Mrs. Isabelle Fox of Sherman Oaks, senior mental health consultant of Operation Head Start, was one of the counselors who dealt with many of the badly upset children and adults. She told us that sleeplessness became a problem for hundreds of people. Many children insisted on sleeping with their parents for months after the earthquake. One man was so affected that he slept in his clothes in the living room after the earthquake, and it was two years before he was able to return to normal sleeping habits.

One young mother suffered emotional problems because of the way she had reacted to the emergency. When the earthquake came, she hid under a table until it was over; only then did she realize that she had left her baby—an adopted child—alone during the earthquake. He was safe and unharmed, but she suffered from guilt feelings because she had thought of herself first. She had been trying to be a perfect mother, and she could not forgive herself for her actions (which were quite normal). Another woman suffered mental distress, sufficiently acute to require psychological help, because all the dishes given her by her deceased mother were broken; she saw this loss as destroying her ties with a beloved one.

Mental depression is another reaction to an earthquake, because the frightening events can reawaken earlier sad and upsetting experiences. Single parents generally suffered more than did couples, perhaps because they had total responsibility for their homes and children. Some adults, unable to work because of mental distress caused by the earthquake, received disability compensation.

A common source of fear reported to Mrs. Fox was the noise accompanying the earthquake. As the earth moves and buildings are damaged, the noise can be deafening, an aspect of earthquakes that is not often anticipated. Many children said it was like the "roar of an animal coming to get them."

Most of the seriously disturbed children, Mrs. Fox reported, were three to twelve years old. Those two years old and younger seemed to be relatively unaffected (perhaps they were unaware of the danger), and most teenagers took the earthquake in stride (perhaps they like excitement). Typical reactions of those who suffered emotional distress were nightmares, waking up screaming, and anxiety attacks. Increased separation anxiety was observed; for instance, some children could not tolerate being left alone when parents needed to leave the house.

To help children recover emotionally from the earthquake, Mrs. Fox devised an ingenious scheme. She had them build a house of blocks on a table; then they shook the table to show what an earthquake does. When parts of the house fell over, the children could see what happened during an earthquake. Then they rebuilt the house, to show that it is possible to recover from disaster. With this kind of understanding, they could reestablish their own security and hasten their return to normalcy. Important to the emotional recovery of both children and adults was the opportunity to talk about their experiences and relive the events that had disturbed them.

A surprising number of people who suffered from the San Fernando earthquake had no prior knowledge of the causes and effects of earthquakes. Lack of knowledge, and in some instances superstitious beliefs, caused them unnecessary distress. Some reported that they believed God was punishing them for real or imagined misdeeds; others thought California "was going to fall into the sea." Presumably they meant the entire state, not just a few houses on seaside bluffs. Small wonder that they were scared! A little education about earthquakes would help such people to keep calm and avoid emotional after-effects.

Psychological preparation for an earthquake can help significantly. Just as fire drills instill an automatic reaction—walk, don't run, to the nearest exit, and remain calm—so also can earthquake drills teach people to react automatically. School children can follow a scenario something like this: The room is beginning to sway, the light fixtures are moving back and forth, the teacher calls out "earthquake." The children immediately hide under their desks, covering their faces with their hands. They keep away from windows and they don't run outside. As another exercise, pictures could be painted showing how the classroom would look during an earthquake, and stories could be written describing what to do.

In Japan, the children are taught at an early age about earthquakes— what they are, what they feel like, and how they affect buildings. Mobile vans, outfitted like a Japanese living room, visit the schools. Several children enter the van, which then is shaken mechanically to simulate an earthquake. This training proves invaluable when they are confronted with the real thing.

Individual Earthquake Preparedness

On the following pages we list a number of things that people can do before, during, and after an earthquake. These suggestions are aimed primarily toward safety at home and work and certainly are not all-inclusive. However, by studying the lists you will get a good idea of the kinds of problems that are created by earthquakes; then you can develop a personal list in accord with your own circumstances and surroundings. The front of your telephone book also contains valuable information about preparing for emergencies and disasters.

Remember that you are much more likely to remain calm and react sensibly if you have thought about your response in advance. A good

A special wrench for opening and closing gas lines is commercially available, although any ordinary wrench will do. (Courtesy of Dave Hedman and Ron Mason, Earthquake Safety Organization, Palo Alto)

Water heaters are heavy (50 gallons of water weighs 400 pounds) and often tear loose from their supports during earthquakes. Flexible metal straps available from hardware stores can be used to tie the tanks to the wall. (Courtesy of Dave Hedman and Ron Mason, Earthquake Safety Organization, Palo Alto)

mental exercise is to think purposefully about what you would do in the next earthquake; you can do this during idle moments at home, at work, in stores, on the street, in a car, in the dentist's waiting room. This kind of "practice" with an imaginary earthquake is excellent preparation for the real event. When an actual earthquake comes, you will be amazed at how quickly you move to a protected place, while others not mentally prepared will be shouting and running about.

What To Do Before the Next Earthquake

This list describes preparations that can be made before the next earthquake. Some of them involve simple actions that everyone should take as soon as possible; others are for those who wish to have greater security.

1. Store drinking water and canned food at home so that you can survive for a few days on your own. One gallon of water per person per day is suggested for drinking and cooking purposes. If the electricity goes out, food in the refrigerator will soon spoil, so canned and dried food will be needed. An emergency method of cooking is convenient; for example, a camp stove or barbecue.

2. Always have flashlights and spare batteries readily available. Keep a flashlight beside your bed.

3. Keep a battery-operated radio at home and at any other places where you spend a great amount of time.

4. Keep one or more fire extinguishers in convenient locations. Keep garden hoses attached to faucets (if water pressure is adequate, they can be used immediately in the event of a fire).

5. Learn how to turn off the gas, electricity, and water at your home and other places where you spend a great amount of time. Keep a wrench of the proper size near the gas shut-off valve.

6. Keep basic first-aid supplies on hand and have a knowledge of first-aid procedures. (After a major disaster, hospitals may be overcrowded and medical personnel may be occupied with more serious cases.) Keep an ample supply of any special medicines that are needed by you or others who live with you.

7. Write the telephone numbers for ambulance, fire, and police services beside your phone.

8. Fasten to the walls any bookcases or other heavy pieces of furniture that might topple and cause injuries. Be sure that heavy equipment is properly fastened to floors and walls.

9. Put one or more straps around water heaters and gas furnaces and attach them securely to the walls. Bolt the supports to the floor.

10. Store dangerous materials, such as flammable liquids and poisons, in a secure place where they cannot fall and break open. Remove heavy objects from upper shelves and store them on the floor or on bottom shelves.

11. Be sure your bed is not located near a large glass window.

12. Make sure that all members of your household, as well as co-workers and others, know what to do during and after an earthquake.

13. If you have small children, tell them what to do if they are in school during an earthquake. (It is usually best if they stay at school until you can go and get them.)

14. Keep a canteen of water at your place of work if there is a chance you will have to walk or bicycle a long distance to reach home after the earthquake is over.

15. Determine whether you live or work in an area that could be subjected to flooding (from a dam failure), landslides, or tsunami damage. If you do, then plan evacuation procedures with members of your household, neighbors, and co-workers. Decide in advance where your family will meet if the neighborhood is evacuated.

16. In the normal course of daily activities at work or school, avoid blocking corridors, doorways, and exits with supplies, bicycles, cars, etc. When an emergency occurs, it is essential that all passages be clear both for evacuation of occupants and for the entry of rescue workers.

17. To protect your home if damage occurs, have available some plywood and sheets of plastic to cover broken windows and other openings.

18. When building or remodeling a house, be sure to provide adequate bracing against horizontal forces. Make sure that the foundations are adequate and that the house is securely tied to the foundation.

19. Support community programs to prepare for earthquakes and other disasters. Support efforts to improve building codes. Support zoning regulations that control the kinds of construction permitted near known active earthquake faults. Support efforts to remodel and rehabilitate old and unsafe buildings, including the removal or reinforcement of unsafe parapets and cornices.

20. Be aware of developments in earthquake prediction by responsible engineers and scientists, especially those working for the U.S. Geological Survey. When the time comes that reliable predictions can be made, follow the advice of the USGS (or other responsible government agencies).

What To Do During the Earthquake

When the earthquake occurs, the ground will shake perceptibly for a relatively short time—perhaps only for a few seconds, perhaps for as much as a minute in a great earthquake. The motion is apt to be frightening, but you have no choice except to wait for it to end. So it is very important to remain calm and in control of yourself. If you act calmly and deliberately you will increase your chances of being safe from harm. Furthermore, other people near you may benefit from your calmness and follow your example.

Act immediately when you feel the ground or building shaking, keeping in mind that the greatest danger is from falling debris. Don't worry about being embarrassed if you hide under a desk or table. The people who wait to see whether or not such action is necessary are the ones who are most likely to be hurt by falling objects.

1. Tell yourself to remain calm and don't do things that upset other people (such as shouting or running around).

2. If you are indoors, move immediately to a safe place. Get under a desk, table, or work bench if possible. Stand in an interior doorway or in the corner of a room. Watch out for falling debris or tall furniture. Stay away from windows, chimneys, and heavy objects (such as refrigerators and machinery) that may topple or slide across the floor.

3. As a general rule, don't run out of a building. Falling debris around a building is a common hazard. It is better to seek safety where you are, wait until the earthquake is over, and then leave calmly if evacuation is necessary.

4. If you are in a tall building, don't rush for stairways or elevators. Exits are likely to be jammed and elevators often stop operating. Seek safety where you are.

5. Don't be surprised if the electricity goes out, or if elevator, fire, and burglar alarms start ringing, or if sprinkler systems go on. Expect to hear noise from breaking glass, cracks in walls, and falling objects.

6. If you are in an unreinforced brick building or other hazardous structure, you may feel it is better to take a chance on leaving the building than to stay inside. Then leave quickly but cautiously, being on the alert for falling bricks, fallen electrical wiring, and other hazards.

7. If you are on the sidewalk near a tall building, step into a door-way to avoid debris falling from the building.

8. If you are outdoors, try to get into an open area, away from buildings and power lines.

9. If you are in a moving automobile, calmly stop the car away from tall buildings, overpasses, and bridges if possible. Remain in the car until the shaking is over.

10. Don't be surprised if you feel more than one shock. After the first motion is felt, there may be a temporary decrease in the motion followed by another shock. This phenomenon is merely the arrival of different seismic waves (first the P wave, then the S wave) from the same earthquake. Also, aftershocks may occur—these are separate earthquakes that follow the main shock. Aftershocks may occur several minutes, several hours, or even several days afterwards. Sometimes aftershocks will cause damage or collapse of structures that were already weakened by the main earthquake.

What To Do After the Earthquake

When the shaking stops, there may be considerable damage and people may be injured. It is especially important that everyone should remain calm and begin the task of taking care of one another. The first concern is for those who are hurt, and the next concern is to prevent fires. After that, damage can be assessed and remedial measures begun.

1. Remain calm, and take time to assess your situation.

2. Help anyone who is hurt. Administer emergency first aid when necessary. Cover injured persons with blankets to keep them warm. Seek medical help for those who need it.

3. Check for fires and fire hazards. Put out fires immediately if you can.

4. Check for damage to utilities and appliances. Shut off gas valves if there is any chance of a gas leak. Detect gas by smell, never by using matches or candles. Shut off electricity if there is any chance of damage to wiring. Shut off water mains if breakage has occurred. In due time, report utility damage to the utility companies and follow their instructions.

5. Do not light matches, use any open flames, or turn on electrical switches or appliances until you are certain there are no gas leaks.

6. Do not touch power lines, electric wiring, or objects in contact with them.

7. Do not use the telephone except to call for help, or to report serious emergencies (injuries, fires, or crimes), or to perform some essential service. Jammed telephone lines interfere with emergency services, and it is thoughtless to use the phone for personal reasons or to satisfy curiosity. (When the emergency is clearly over, contact relatives and friends so they will know you are safe and where you are.)

8. Do not go sightseeing nor occupy the streets unnecessarily. Do not visit damaged areas unless your assistance is needed. Avoid beach areas where seismic sea waves (tsunamis) could arrive.

9. Before resuming use of toilets, be certain that sewer lines are not broken.

10. Wear sturdy shoes in order not to be injured by broken glass or other sharp debris.

11. Clean up and warn others of any spilled materials that are dangerous, such as chemicals and gasoline.

12. Listen to the radio for information about the earthquake and disaster procedures.

13. Be prepared to experience aftershocks. They often do additional damage to buildings weakened by the main shock.

14. Use great caution when entering or moving about in a damaged building. Collapses can occur without much warning, and there may be dangers from gas leaks, electric wiring, broken glass, etc.

15. If electricity is out, use up foods from the refrigerator that will spoil, then turn to canned and dried foods. Use camp stoves and barbecues for emergency cooking.

16. Inspect chimneys for damage; do not use fireplaces unless the chimney is undamaged and without cracks.

17. Open closet doors and cupboards cautiously because objects may fall outward on you.

18. Be reassuring and helpful to young children and others who may suffer psychological trauma from the earthquake. Do not spread rumors.

19. If you are at home during the earthquake, assist your family and neighbors in coping with the damage. When you have done what you can, consider how you can help at nearby places such as schools or places of work. If you are at work when the earthquake strikes, assist in every way you can there; then make your way home.

20. Cooperate with police, fire, paramedical, and other people engaged in rescue and repair work.

Earthquakes will always cause death, injury, and destruction, and no rules can make us completely safe. Furthermore, some rules will apply only in certain situations and must be altered or abandoned under other circumstances. However, by judicious use of the preceding suggestions you can greatly reduce the dangers from earthquakes and be of more help to yourself and others when the next disaster strikes.

Table A-1
Earthquake Data

Richter Magnitude	Average Number of Earthquakes per Year for the World	Average Number of Earthquakes per 100 Years for California	Duration of Strong Ground Shaking (seconds)	Radius of Region Subjected to Strong Ground Shaking (kilometers)
8.0 to 8.9	1	1	30 to 90	80 to 160
7.0 to 7.9	15	12	20 to 50	50 to 120
6.0 to 6.9	140	80	10 to 30	20 to 80
5.0 to 5.9	900	400	2 to 15	5 to 30
4.0 to 4.9	8,000	2,000	0 to 5	0 to 15

Table A-2
Significant Earthquakes of the World

Date	Location	Magnitude	Deaths	Remarks
c.1250 B.C.	Mt. Sinai			The "whole Mount quaked greatly" as Moses was about to receive the Ten Commandments. —Exodus 19:18.
780 B.C.	China; Shaanxi Province			Widespread destruction west of Xian.
373 B.C.	Greece			Helice, on the Gulf of Corinth, was destroyed. Much of the city slid into the sea.
70 B.C.	China; Shandong Province		6,000	
63 A.D.	Italy; near Mt. Vesuvius			Earthquakes continued for 16 years, culminating with the famous eruption on Aug. 24, 79 that buried Pompeii and Herculaneum.
342	Turkey		40,000	Antioch destroyed.
365 July 21	Eastern Mediterranean region		50,000	Major destruction on Crete. Tsunami drowned 5,000 people in Alexandria.
551 July 9	Lebanon			Beirut destroyed.
844 Sept. 18	Syria		50,000	Damascus destroyed.
856 Dec.	Northern Africa and the Middle East		45,000	Many cities destroyed from Tunisia to Iran.
893	India		180,000	Widespread damage.
1038 Jan. 9	China; Shanxi Province	7.3	32,000	Many villages destroyed in the region north of Taiyuan.
1068 Mar. 18	Palestine		25,000	Many villages destroyed.
1138 Sept. 8	Syria		100,000	Aleppo destroyed.
1202 May 20	Middle East		30,000	Felt over an area of 800,000 square miles, including Egypt, Syria, Asia Minor, Sicily, Armenia, and Azerbaijan. Variously reported as occurring in 1201 or 1202 with over a million deaths (which is highly improbable).

Note: Although the number of deaths for ancient earthquakes is taken from the earthquake literature, we believe the figures are highly exaggerated.

Continued on next page

Date	Location	Magnitude	Deaths	Remarks
1293 May 20	Japan; Kanagawa Prefecture		30,000	Major destruction in Kamakura.
1303 Sept. 17	China; Shanxi Province	8.0	15,000	Major destruction in Hongdong and vicinity.
1455 Dec. 5	Italy		40,000	Naples badly damaged.
1531 Jan. 26	Portugal; Lisbon		30,000	
1556 Jan. 23	China; Shaanxi Province	8.0	830,000	Greatest natural disaster in history. Occurred at night in the densely populated region around Xian. Thousands of landslides on the hillsides, which consist of soft rock. Many peasants living in caves were killed. Many villages destroyed and thousands of deaths when houses collapsed.
1626 July 30	Italy; Naples		70,000	
1667 Nov.	U.S.S.R.; Azerbaijan		80,000	
1668 July 25	China; Shandong Province	8.5	50,000	Widespread destruction throughout province.
1688 July 5	Turkey		15,000	Damage along Aegean coast.
1692 June 7	Jamaica; Port Royal		2,000	Large section of the city subsided into the sea.
1693 Jan. 9	Sicily		60,000	Catania destroyed.
1695 May 18	China; Shanxi Province	8.0	30,000	
1703 Dec. 30	Japan; Tokyo region	8.2	5,200	Tsunami.
1715	Algeria		20,000	Algiers destroyed.
1727 Nov. 18	Iran; Tabrīz		77,000	
1730 Dec. 30	Japan; Hokkaidō Prefecture		137,000	
1737 Oct. 11	India; Calcutta		300,000	

Continued on next page

Date	Location	Magnitude	Deaths	Remarks
1739 Jan. 3	China; Ningxia Province	8.0	50,000	
1746 Oct. 28	Peru	8.4	5,000	Destruction in Lima. Tsunami.
1755 Nov. 1	Portugal; Lisbon	8.6	60,000	All Saints' Day; many killed when churches collapsed and fire ravaged the city. Large tsunami killed many.
1757 Aug. 6	Sicily; Syracuse		10,000	
1759 Oct. 30	Lebanon; Baalbek		30,000	Famous Roman temples destroyed.
1783 Feb. 5	Italy; Calabria		50,000	First earthquake to be investigated scientifically.
1792 May 21	Japan; Kyūshū Island		15,000	
1797 Feb. 4	Ecuador		41,000	Quito destroyed.
1811 Dec. 16	U.S.A.; New Madrid, Missouri	7.5		Sequence of three large earthquakes. Caused major changes in topography, creating lakes and altering the course of rivers. Felt in Boston, 1100 miles away. Because of remote location, only a few deaths.
1812 Jan. 23	U.S.A.; New Madrid Missouri	7.3		
1812 Feb. 7	U.S.A.; New Madrid, Missouri	7.8		
1812 Mar. 25	Venezuela; Caracas		20,000	City destroyed.
1815 Nov. 27	Indonesia; Bali		10,200	
1828 Dec. 18	Japan; Honshū Island	6.9	30,000	Damage in Echigo region (now Niigata Prefecture).
1835 Feb. 20	Chile; Concepción	8.5		Described by Charles Darwin, who was on shore, in *The Voyage of the Beagle*. Large ground displacements. Tsunami.
1837	Syria and Palestine		5,000	Damascus and Beirut damaged.
1847 May 8	Japan; Honshū Island	7.4	12,000	
1850 Sept. 12	China; Sichuan Province	7.5	21,000	

Continued on next page

Date	Location	Magnitude	Deaths	Remarks
1855 Nov. 11	Japan; Honshū Island	6.9	7,000	Great fire in Edo (now Tokyo).
1857 Jan. 9	U.S.A.; Fort Tejon, California	8.3	1	San Andreas fault offset about 30 feet; fault ruptured for 250 miles. Because of remote location, only one known death.
1857 Dec. 16	Italy; Naples	6.5	12,000	
1859 June 2	Turkey	6.1	15,000	
1861 Mar. 10	Argentina; Mendoza	7.5	8,000	Mendoza destroyed.
1863 July 2	Philippines; Manila		10,000	
1868 Aug. 13	Chile and Peru	8.5	25,000	Large tsunami devastated Arica (now in Chile, but then in Peru).
1868 Aug. 16	Ecuador and Colombia		70,000	
1872 Mar. 26	U.S.A.; Owens Valley, California	8.5	27	One of the strongest U.S. earthquakes. Created fault scarp 20 feet high.
1875 May 16	Colombia		10,000	Many villages destroyed.
1883 Aug. 26	Indonesia; Java		36,000	
1883 Oct. 15	Greece		15,000	
1891 Oct. 28	Japan; Nobi Plain	7.9	7,300	Also known as Mino-Owari earthquake (Mino and Owari Provinces are now part of Gifu Prefecture). Many buildings destroyed. Large ground displacements.
1893 Nov. 17	U.S.S.R.; Turkmenistan		18,000	
1896 June 15	Japan; off the Sanriku coast	7.5	27,000	Large tsunami swept the coast and engulfed entire villages.
1897 June 12	India; Assam	8.7	1,500	Large fault scarp formed (vertical displacement 35 feet). Much building damage in Shillong.
1905 Apr. 4	India; Punjab-Kashmir region	8.6	19,000	Great length of faulting. Kangra destroyed.
1905 Sept. 8	Italy; Calabria	7.9	557	

Continued on next page

Date	Location	Magnitude	Deaths	Remarks
1906 Jan. 31	Ecuador (off the coast)	8.9	1,000	One of the largest earthquakes of record. Lasted over three minutes.
1906 Apr. 18	U.S.A.; San Francisco, California	8.3	700	San Andreas fault ruptured for 270 miles. Great fire burned much of the city.
1906 Aug. 16	Chile; near Valparaíso	8.6	1,500	Changes of ground level at the coast.
1907 Jan. 14	Jamaica	6.5	1,000	Damage at Kingston.
1907 Oct. 21	U.S.S.R.; Tadzhikistan	8.1	12,000	
1908 Dec. 28	Italy; Straits of Messina	7.5	58,000	Messina destroyed.
1909 Jan. 23	Iran (west-central)	7.3	5,500	
1915 Jan. 13	Italy; Avezzano	7.5	32,600	
1917 Jan. 21	Indonesia; Bali		15,000	
1918 Feb. 13	China; Guangdong Province	7.3	10,000	
1918 Oct. 11	Puerto Rico (western)	7.5	116	Tsunami caused several deaths.
1920 Jan. 3	Mexico; west of Veracruz	7.8	648	
1920 Sept. 7	Italy; Reggio di Calabria		1,400	Severe damage.
1920 Dec. 16	China; Ningxia Province	8.6	200,000	Many landslides covered villages and towns.
1923 Mar. 24	China; Sichuan Province	7.3	5,000	
1923 May 26	Iran (north-eastern)	5.5	2,200	
1923 Sept. 1	Japan; Tokyo	8.3	99,300	Known as Kanto earthquake. Major damage over a large area, including Tokyo and Yokohama. Great fire in Tokyo. Large tsunami inundated coastal regions.
1927 Mar. 7	Japan; Tango Peninsula	7.8	3,020	Town of Mineyama totally destroyed.
1927 May 23	China; Gansu Province	8.3	41,000	

Continued on next page

Date	Location	Magnitude	Deaths	Remarks
1929 May 1	Iran (north-eastern)	7.2	5,800	
1930 May 7	Iran (north-western)	7.2	2,510	
1930 July 23	Italy; Campania	6.5	1,425	Extensive damage near Ariano Irpino.
1931 Feb. 3	New Zealand; Hawke Bay	7.8	225	Many buildings damaged in Napier.
1933 Mar. 3	Japan; off the Sanriku coast	8.9	3,000	One of the largest earthquakes of record. Large tsunami caused much damage and loss of life.
1934 Jan. 15	India; Bihar	8.4	10,700	Much land subsidence.
1935 Apr. 21	Taiwan	7.1	3,276	Extensive faulting.
1935 June 1	Pakistan; Quetta	7.6	25,000	City destroyed.
1939 Jan. 24	Chile; Chillán	8.3	28,000	City destroyed; 100,000 people homeless.
1939 Dec. 27	Turkey; Erzincan	8.0	32,700	Many communities destroyed.
1940 Nov. 10	Romania; Vrancea district	7.4	1,000	Severe damage to buildings in Bucharest.
1942 Nov. 26	Turkey	7.6	4,000	
1943 Sept. 10	Japan; Tottori and Okayama Prefectures	7.4	1,190	Epicenter near city of Tottori.
1944 Jan. 15	Argentina; San Juan	7.8	5,000	City devastated.
1944 Dec. 7	Japan; Wakayama Prefecture	8.3	1,000	Known as Tonankai earthquake. Tsunami.
1945 Jan. 13	Japan; Aichi Prefecture	7.1	1,960	Epicenter in Mikawa Bay.
1945 Nov. 28	Pakistan (off the coast)	8.3	4,100	Tsunami.
1946 Nov. 10	Peru; Ancash	7.4	1,400	Great landslides.
1946 Dec. 21	Japan; south of Shikoku Island	8.4	1,360	Known as the Nankai earthquake. Great tsunami.
1948 June 28	Japan; Fukui Prefecture	7.3	5,400	Only known instance of a person being crushed in a ground fissure.

Continued on next page

Date	Location	Magnitude	Deaths	Remarks
1948 Oct. 6	U.S.S.R.; Turkmenistan	7.3	19,800	Serious damage to Ashkhabad.
1949 Aug. 5	Ecuador (central)	6.8	6,000	Many villages destroyed.
1950 Aug. 15	India; Assam (eastern)	8.7	150	Damage in region along border with Tibet. Landslides and floods.
1952 Mar. 4	Japan; Hokkaidō	8.3	31	Known as the Tokachi-Oki earthquake. Tsunami.
1953 Mar. 18	Turkey (northwestern)	7.5	1,100	
1954 Sept. 9	Algeria; El Asnam	6.8	1,240	El Asnam (then Orléansville) destroyed.
1957 July 28	Mexico; Guerrero	7.9	68	Tall buildings damaged in Mexico City, 180 miles away.
1960 Feb. 29	Morocco; Agadir	5.7	12,000	One-third of population of Agadir killed. Most of the city destroyed.
1960 May 22	Chile; off the coast near Concepción	8.5	2,230	Tsunami caused 61 deaths in Hilo, Hawaii and 120 deaths in Japan. Travel time of tsunami from Chile to Japan (11,000 miles) was 22 hours.
1962 Sept. 1	Iran (northwestern); Qazvin	7.3	12,200	
1963 July 26	Yugoslavia; Skopje	6.0	1,070	Many buildings damaged or collapsed.
1964 Mar. 27	U.S.A.; Prince William Sound, Alaska	8.4	131	Known as the Good Friday earthquake. Severe damage to Anchorage and other cities. Landslides. Great tsunami damaged many coastal cities in Alaska and killed 11 people in Crescent City, California.
1964 June 16	Japan; Niigata	7.5	26	Liquefaction and subsidence caused much building damage. Large tsunami caused coastal flooding.
1967 July 29	Venezuela; Caracas	6.5	266	Many buildings damaged. Several high-rise buildings collapsed.
1967 Dec. 11	India; Koyna Dam	6.4	177	Caused by filling of the reservoir. Village of Koyna Naga heavily damaged.
1968 Jan. 14	Sicily (western)	6.1	740	Seventeen earthquakes with magnitudes 4.1 to 6.1 from Jan. 14 to Feb. 6.

Continued on next page

Date	Location	Magnitude	Deaths	Remarks
1968 May 16	Japan; Hachinohe (off the coast)	8.6	48	Known as the Tokachi-Oki earthquake. Damage to many buildings and port facilities from tsunami.
1968 Aug. 31	Iran (eastern); Khorāsān	7.3	12,100	About 60,000 people homeless.
1969 Feb. 23	Indonesia; Celebes	6.9	600	
1969 July 26	China; Guang-dong Province	5.9	3,000	
1970 Mar. 28	Turkey; Gediz	7.3	1,100	Many buildings collapsed.
1970 May 31	Peru; Chimbote	7.8	67,000	Greatest earthquake disaster in the Western Hemisphere. About 800,000 people homeless. Huge landslide on Mt. Huascarán buried 18,000 people in Ranrahirca and Yungay.
1972 Apr. 10	Iran (south-central)	7.1	5,400	Village of Qir destroyed.
1972 Dec. 23	Nicaragua; Managua	6.2	5,000	Extensive building damage.
1973 Aug. 28	Mexico; northern Oaxaca	7.2	530	Many houses destroyed.
1974 May 11	China; Yunnan Province	7.1	20,000	
1974 Oct. 3	Peru; Lima	7.6	78	Extensive damage in Lima.
1974 Dec. 28	Kashmir	6.0	700	Villages destroyed.
1975 Feb. 4	China; Liaoning Province; Haicheng	7.3	1,300	Earthquake successfully predicted and population evacuated. Heavy damage, but many lives saved.
1975 Sept. 6	Turkey; Lice	6.7	2,370	Seventy-five percent of the buildings in Lice destroyed.
1976 Feb. 4	Guatemala	7.5	23,000	Extensive damage to adobe-type buildings. Numerous landslides. One-fifth of the population homeless.
1976 May 6	Italy; Friuli region (near Gemona)	6.5	965	Extensive damage; many buildings destroyed.
1976 June 26	New Guinea (west)	7.1	6,000	Villages destroyed. Landslides.

Continued on next page

Date	Location	Magnitude	Deaths	Remarks
1976 July 14	Indonesia; Bali	6.5	560	
1976 July 28	China; Hebei Province; Tangshan	7.8	243,000	Major industrial city totally destroyed. Four aftershocks on same day with magnitudes 6.5, 6.0, 7.1, and 6.0.
1976 Aug. 17	Philippines; Moro Gulf	8.0	6,500	Many buildings damaged. Large tsunami.
1976 Nov. 24	Turkey (eastern)	7.3	5,000	Many buildings collapsed in Muradiye and Caldiran.
1977 Mar. 4	Romania; Vrancea district	7.2	1,570	Many buildings collapsed in Bucharest.
1977 Nov. 23	Argentina; San Juan Province; Caucete	7.4	70	Extensive damage to village.
1978 June 12	Japan; Sendai	7.5	27	A few modern buildings damaged.
1978 Sept. 16	Iran (central); Tabas	7.7	15,000	In Tabas, 9,000 out of 13,000 population killed.
1978 Nov. 29	Mexico; Oaxaca	7.8	8	Many buildings damaged.
1979 Apr. 15	Yugoslavia; southern Montenegro	7.0	156	Near the Adriatic coast. Extensive damage.
1979 Sept. 12	New Guinea (west)	8.1	100	Near island of Yapen.
1979 Dec. 12	Colombia (southwestern coast)	7.7	600	Off the coast. Large tsunami.
1980 Oct. 10	Algeria; El Asnam	7.3	5,000	Large fault scarps. Many buildings collapsed; 200,000 people homeless. El Asnam 60 percent destroyed.
1980 Nov. 23	Italy (southern)	7.0	3,100	Several large shocks. Great damage to homes built of stone masonry in Calabritto and nearby towns.
1981 June 11	Iran (southeastern); near Kermān	6.9	3,000	Town of Golbaf severely damaged.
1981 July 28	Iran (southeastern); near Kermān	7.3	2,500	Town of Sirch severely damaged; 50,000 people homeless.
1981 Sept. 12	Kashmir	6.1	212	Many houses damaged.

Continued on next page

Date	Location	Magnitude	Deaths	Remarks
1982 June 7	Mexico; Guerrero	7.2	9	A second earthquake of magnitude 7.0 on same day. Damage as far away as Mexico City.
1982 June 19	El Salvador	7.0	16	Rural villages damaged.
1982 Dec. 13	Yemen; east of Sanaa	6.0	2,800	Many villages destroyed. Landslides in mountainous regions.
1982 Dec. 16	Afghanistan; north of Kābul	6.8	510	Extensive damage in Hindu Kush region.
1983 Mar. 31	Colombia	5.5	350	Widespread damage in Popayán. Many buildings collapsed. Thousands homeless.
1983 May 25	Japan; Honshū Island	7.7	106	Tsunami struck the coast near Akita and caused 105 deaths.
1983 Oct. 30	Turkey	6.9	2,000	Many villages destroyed in eastern Turkey.

Table A-3

Significant Earthquakes of the United States

Date	Location	Mag-nitude	In-tensity	Remarks
1663 Feb. 5	St. Lawrence River region		X	Rockslides near Three Rivers, Quebec. Chimneys fell in Massachusetts Bay region.
1755 Nov. 18	Off Cape Ann, Massachusetts	6.0	VIII	Chimneys fell and buildings damaged in Boston and elsewhere. Many ships at sea were jolted.
1811 Dec. 16	New Madrid, Missouri	7.5	XII	Sequence of three large earthquakes caused major changes in topography, creating lakes and altering the course of rivers. Felt in Boston, 1100 miles away. Because of remote location only a few deaths.
1812 Jan. 23	New Madrid, Missouri	7.3	XII	
1812 Feb. 7	New Madrid, Missouri	7.8	XII	
1836 June 10	Hayward, California	8.0	X	Extensive surface rupture on Hayward fault. Numerous aftershocks. Buildings collapsed.
1838 June	San Francisco peninsula	8.2	X	Extensive surface rupture on San Andreas fault from San Francisco to Santa Clara.
1857 Jan. 9	Fort Tejon, California	8.3	XI	San Andreas fault offset about 30 feet; fault ruptured for 250 miles. Because of remote location, only one known death.
1868 Apr. 2	Island of Hawaii	7.7	X	Volcanic earthquake on south slope of Mauna Loa. Much damage to houses. Tsunami killed 46 people.
1868 Oct. 21	Hayward, California	7.5	IX	Extensive surface rupture on Hayward fault. 30 deaths. Many aftershocks.
1872 Mar. 26	Owens Valley, California	8.5	XI	One of the strongest U.S. earthquakes. Fault scarp 20 feet high. 27 deaths.
1886 Aug. 31	Charleston, South Carolina	7.0	X	Greatest earthquake in eastern U.S. Several aftershocks. Much building damage. 110 deaths.
1895 Oct. 31	Charleston, Missouri		VIII	Chimneys fell. Earthquake felt from Canada to Louisiana.
1899 Sept. 3	Near Cape Yakataga, Alaska	8.3	XI	Ground uplifts; seiches; people unable to stand.
1899 Sept. 10	Yakutat Bay, Alaska	8.6	XI	Glaciers broken up. Large waves. Shoreline rose 45 feet.
1900 Oct. 9	Chugach Mountains, Alaska	8.3	VIII	Buildings damaged at Kodiak.

Continued on next page

Date	Location	Magnitude	Intensity	Remarks
1906 Apr. 18	San Francisco, California	8.3	XI	San Andreas fault ruptured for 270 miles. Ground offset 21 feet. About 700 deaths during earthquake and fire.
1915 Oct. 2	Pleasant Valley, Nevada	7.6	X	Large fault displacements in an unpopulated region. Adobe houses destroyed.
1918 Oct. 11	Puerto Rico	7.5	IX	Epicenter in Mona Passage. Many buildings destroyed. Tsunami caused much damage. 116 deaths.
1922 Mar. 10	Cholame Valley, California	6.5	IX	Ground cracks; damage to houses.
1925 Feb. 28	St. Lawrence River region	7.0	VIII	Felt as far south as Virginia and west to the Mississippi River.
1925 June 27	Manhattan, Montana	6.7	VIII	Buildings damaged. Rockslides.
1925 June 29	Santa Barbara, California	6.3	IX	Much building damage. Sheffield Dam failed. 13 deaths.
1927 Nov. 4	Point Arguello, California	7.5	X	Epicenter off the coast. Landslides near Santa Barbara. Tsunami recorded in Hawaii.
1929 Oct. 5	Island of Hawaii	6.5	VII	Near Kailua (Kona). Walls fell.
1931 Aug. 16	Valentine, Texas	6.4	VIII	Buildings damaged; chimneys fell.
1932 June 6	Humboldt County, California	6.4	VIII	Epicenter off the coast. Buildings cracked in Eureka. 1 death.
1932 Dec. 20	Cedar Mountain, Nevada	7.3	X	Region was uninhabited at the time. Many ground fissures.
1933 Mar. 10	Long Beach, California	6.3	IX	Much damage to buildings, especially schools. 120 deaths.
1934 Jan. 30	Excelsior Mountains, Nevada	6.5	VIII	Minor surface faulting. Minor damage in Mina.
1934 Mar. 12	Kosmo, Utah	6.6	VIII	Many ground changes (fissures, rockslides, new springs). Chimneys fell. 2 deaths.
1935 Oct. 18	Helena, Montana	6.2	VIII	Many buildings damaged. 2 deaths. Strong aftershock on Oct. 31 (magnitude 6.0) caused 2 additional deaths.
1940 May 18	El Centro, California	7.1	X	Large ground displacements along Imperial fault. Much building damage. 9 deaths. First important accelerogram for engineering use.

Continued on next page

Date	Location	Magnitude	Intensity	Remarks
1944 Sept. 4	Northern New York State	5.6	VIII	Chimneys damaged.
1946 Apr. 1	Aleutian Islands (south of Unimak Island)	7.5	VI	Large tsunami struck Hilo, Hawaii, killing 96 people and causing much building damage. 173 deaths.
1947 Nov. 23	Southwestern Montana	6.2	VIII	Buildings damaged in Virginia City and nearby towns.
1949 Apr. 13	Olympia, Washington	7.3	VIII	Many buildings damaged. 8 deaths.
1951 Aug. 21	Island of Hawaii	6.8	IX	Many buildings damaged along Kona coast. Minor damage from tsunami.
1952 July 21	Kern County, California	7.7	XI	Railroad tunnel collapsed; buildings damaged at Tehachapi. Many large aftershocks. 12 deaths.
1952 Aug. 22	Bakersfield, California	5.8	VIII	Damage to buildings. 2 deaths.
1954 Dec. 16	Fairview Peak, Nevada	7.1	X	Large fault scarps. Because of remote location, no deaths. Reservoir in Sacramento, 185 miles away, badly damaged by sloshing water.
1954 Dec. 16	Dixie Valley, Nevada	6.8	X	Occurred four minutes after preceding earthquake; epicenter 40 miles north.
1954 Dec. 21	Eureka, California	6.6	VII	Minor building damage; many pipeline breaks. One death.
1957 Mar. 9	Aleutian Islands (south of Adak)	8.3	VIII	Houses and bridges damaged on Adak Island. Tsunami caused damage on the islands of Oahu and Kauai.
1957 Mar. 22	Daly City, California	5.3	VII	Minor building damage.
1958 Apr. 7	Alaska (central)	7.3	VIII	Pressure ridges; ground cracks.
1958 July 9	Lituya Bay, Alaska	7.9	XI	Earthquake on Fairweather fault. Massive landslide created a huge water wave. 5 deaths.
1959 Aug. 17	Hebgen Lake, Montana	7.7	X	Huge landslide dammed Madison River and formed "Earthquake Lake." Seiche in Hebgen Lake. Houses and roads damaged. Many aftershocks. 28 deaths.
1964 Mar. 27	Prince William Sound, Alaska	8.4	XI	Known as the Good Friday earthquake. Severe damage to Anchorage and many other cities. Landslides. Great tsunami damaged many coastal cities in Alaska and killed 11 people in Crescent City, California. 131 deaths.

Continued on next page

Date	Location	Mag-nitude	In-tensity	Remarks
1965 Apr. 29	Puget Sound, Washington	6.6	VIII	Buildings damaged in Seattle, Tacoma, and vicinity. 6 deaths.
1969 Oct. 1	Santa Rosa, California	5.7	VIII	Much building damage. Second shock an hour later of same magnitude.
1971 Feb. 9	San Fernando, California	6.6	XI	Several buildings and highway bridges collapsed. Many instrumental records obtained. 58 deaths.
1972 July 30	Sitka, Alaska	7.6	VII	Minor damage.
1973 Apr. 26	Island of Hawaii	6.2	VIII	North of Hilo. Damage to buildings and roads in and around Hilo.
1975 June 30	Yellowstone National Park, Wyoming	6.4	VII	Rockfalls; new geysers formed.
1975 Aug. 1	Oroville, California	5.9	VIII	Minor damage to buildings.
1975 Nov. 29	Island of Hawaii	7.2	VIII	Volcanic earthquake near Kalapana (on south coast). Much building damage. Landslides. Tsunami caused damage along coast. 2 deaths.
1978 Aug. 13	Santa Barbara, California	5.7	VIII	Moderate building damage; train derailed.
1979 Oct. 15	Imperial Valley, California	6.7	VII	Extensive surface rupture on Imperial fault. Damage to buildings and canals.
1980 May 18	Mount St. Helens, Washington	5.2		Volcanic earthquake. Preceded a major eruption that killed 60 people.
1980 May 25	Mammoth Lakes, California	6.1	VII	Three earthquakes of magnitudes greater than 6.0 from May 25 to 27. Many smaller shocks. Many rockslides in the Sierra Nevada.
1980 July 27	Northern Kentucky	5.3	VII	Minor building damage.
1980 Nov. 8	Eureka, California	7.4	VII	Off the coast. Highway bridge collapsed; moderate building damage. Five people injured.
1983 May 2	Coalinga, California	6.5	VIII	Many old buildings destroyed. 45 people injured. 1 death.
1983 Oct. 28	Idaho	6.9		Buildings damaged in Mackay and Challis. 2 deaths.
1984 Apr. 24	Mt. Hamilton, California	6.2		On the Calaveras fault, 12 miles east of San Jose. Numerous homes and buildings damaged. Minor injuries.

Additional Reading

1. Ballard, Robert D., *Exploring Our Living Planet*, National Geographic Society, Washington, D.C., 1983, 366 pp. (A fascinating description of the earth, including geology, plate tectonics, earthquakes, volcanism, mountain building, and much more. Amply illustrated with the high-quality color photographs for which the society's publications are noted.)

2. Bolt, Bruce A., *Earthquakes: A Primer*, W. H. Freeman and Co., San Francisco, 1978, 241 pp. (An excellent presentation for the general reader, yet also authoritative and educational for the serious student. Covers all aspects of earthquakes. Professor Bolt not only possesses a wealth of knowledge about earthquakes, but he also writes with clarity, succinctness, and style.)

3. Bolt, B.A., Horn, W.L., Macdonald, G.A., and Scott, R.F., *Geological Hazards*, 2nd ed., Springer-Verlag, New York, 1977, 330 pp. (Covers earthquakes, volcanoes, tsunamis, landslides, avalanches, and floods. Written for the general reader.)

4. Canby, Thomas Y., "California's San Andreas Fault," *National Geographic Magazine*, vol. 143, no. 1 (January 1973), pp. 38-53. (Describes the fault and its behavior.)

5. Canby, Thomas Y., "Can We Predict Quakes?" *National Geographic Magazine*, vol. 149, no. 6 (June 1976), pp. 830-835. (Describes methods of earthquake prediction.)

6. *Continents Adrift and Continents Aground*, Readings from Scientific American, with introductions by J. Tuzo Wilson, W. H. Freeman and Co., San Francisco, 1976, 230 pp. (Contains reprints of 17 articles on plate tectonics, continental drift, seafloor spreading, and the structure of the earth. Authoritative reading for the serious student.)

7. Eiby, G. A., *Earthquakes*, Van Nostrand Reinhold Co., New York, 1980, 209 pp. (An authoritative and excellent presentation for the serious reader.)

8. Gere, J. M., and Shah, H. C., "A Visit to Tangshan," *The Stanford Engineer*, (Fall/Winter 1980-81), pp. 15-22. (The story of the 1976 Tangshan, China, earthquake.)

9. Graves, William P. E., "Earthquake!" *National Geographic Magazine*, vol. 126, no. 1 (July 1964), pp. 112-139. (The story of the March 27, 1964, Alaska earthquake in words and pictures.)

10. Halacy, D. S., Jr., *Earthquakes*, Bobbs-Merrill Co., Indianapolis, 1974, 162 pp. (A nontechnical book for the general reader.)

11. Heirtzler, J. R., "Where the Earth Turns Inside Out," *National Geographic Magazine*, vol. 147, no. 5 (May 1975), pp. 586-603. (The story of a deep-ocean dive to the Mid-Atlantic Ridge.)

12. *The Home Builder's Guide for Earthquake Design*, Applied Technology Council, Palo Alto, California, 1980, 63 pp. (This booklet gives practical technical information for home builders. Available from the Applied Technology Council, 2471 E. Bayshore Road, Suite 512, Palo Alto, California 94303.)

13. Iacopi, Robert, *Earthquake Country*, Lane Books, Menlo Park, California, 1971, 160 pp. (The story of California's earthquakes and major faults, especially the San Andreas fault. A nontechnical book for the general reader.)

14. Matthews, Samuel W., "This Changing Earth," *National Geographic Magazine*, vol. 143, no. 1 (January 1973), pp. 1-37. (Describes earthquakes, plate movement, seafloor spreading, and other geological effects.)

15. McDowell, Bart, "Earthquake in Guatemala," *National Geographic Magazine*, vol. 149, no. 6 (June 1976), pp. 810-829. (The story of the February 4, 1976, Guatemala earthquake in words and pictures.)

16. Press, Frank, and Siever, Raymond, *Earth*, 3rd ed., W. H. Freeman & Co., San Francisco, 1982, 613 pp. (The definitive textbook on all aspects of the title subject. For students and other serious readers.)

17. Richter, Charles F., *Elementary Seismology*, W. H. Freeman and Co., San Francisco, 1958, 768 pp. (The classic textbook on seismology; essential reading for the college student studying earthquakes.)

18. Rikitake, T., *Earthquake Prediction*, Elsevier Scientific Publishing Co., Amsterdam, 1976, 357 pp. (A technical reference book on the subject; thorough and authoritative.)

19. Thomas, Mrs. Lowell, Jr., "Night of Terror," *National Geographic Magazine*, vol. 126, no. 1 (July 1964), pp. 142-156. (Personal account of survival during the Turnagain Heights landslide in the March 27, 1964, Alaska, earthquake.)

20. Verney, Peter, *The Earthquake Handbook*, Paddington Press, Ltd., New York and London, 1979, 224 pp. (A nontechnical book for the general reader.)

21. Yanev, Peter, *Peace of Mind in Earthquake Country*, Chronicle Books, San Francisco, 1974, 304 pp. (An excellent source of information for the homeowner.)

Other Sources of Information

Books and reports containing general information about earthquakes and their effects are available in many libraries. Specific information, such as a geological study for a particular location, may also be available; inquire at the nearest office of the U.S. Geological Survey, the California Division of Mines and Geology, or your city or county planning office. Professional engineers and geologists sometimes offer consulting services related specifically to seismic design. Also, many cities have disaster centers or emergency operations centers that can supply preparedness assistance.

(Photo by Chuck Painter, courtesy of Stanford News and Publications)

About the Authors

When JAMES M. GERE came to Stanford to study applied mechanics, he had already served an apprenticeship in his father's civil engineering business in Syracuse, New York. He also had received his bachelor's and master's degrees in civil engineering at Rensselaer Polytechnic Institute. By the time he earned his PhD, he was committed to the West and stayed to teach at Stanford, becoming professor of civil engineering in 1962. From 1960 to 1970 he served as associate dean of the School of Engineering and from 1967 to 1972 as chairman of the Department of Civil Engineering.

He then turned his attention to the study of earthquakes and the education and training of earthquake engineers. In 1974, he and Professor Haresh Shah became codirectors of the John A. Blume Earthquake Engineering Center in the Department of Civil Engineering. In the Center's laboratory, graduate students and faculty learn to design safer structures of all kinds.

Author of seven textbooks and numerous articles, Professor Gere is a Fellow of the American Society of Civil Engineers and a member of the Earthquake Engineering Research Institute. When he is not teaching, advising community groups on earthquake preparedness, traveling to earthquake sites, or creating mock earthquakes in the laboratory, Jim Gere is hiking or backpacking in the Sierra Nevada, in remote corners of the Grand Canyon, or on Kauai. He has scrambled to the top of every mountain peak shown in Figure 8-1 of this book. He and his wife, Janice, live on the Stanford campus; they have a daughter and two sons.

International travel began early for HARESH C. SHAH. In 1959 he left his home in Poona, India, to study at Stanford, where he earned his PhD in structural engineering in 1963. After six years on the faculty of the University of Pennsylvania, he returned to teach at Stanford in 1968, where he was responsible for unifying the faculty efforts in earthquake engineering that led to the establishment of the John A. Blume Earthquake Engineering Center. Professor of structural engineering since 1973, Haresh

Shah is much sought after as a consultant to business and professional organizations and to local, state, and national governments.

As advisor to countries in Central and South America, North Africa, Europe, and Asia, Professor Shah has traveled widely—to China three times, and around the world, by last count, five times. He has directly assisted the governments of Nicaragua, Costa Rica, Honduras, Guatemala, and Algeria in coping with earthquake disasters by working with them to develop administrative procedures and building codes, and to further their understanding and expertise in earthquake engineering. He has worked on earthquake-related problems with the National Science Foundation (NSF), UNESCO, NATO, and the United Nations Disaster Relief Organization (UNDRO).

Although he may be in Japan one week and in Washington, D.C., the next, Professor Shah has found time to contribute over 150 articles to the scientific literature, to serve on the board of directors of the Earthquake Engineering Research Institute, and to play a prominent role in other professional organizations.

Haresh Shah is also a hiker and climber, both in the Sierra Nevada and in the Ladakh region of the Himalayas. He and his wife, Joan, live on the Stanford campus with their two sons.

CREDITS

COVER AND COLOR MAP	Design by Tom Lewis, The Design Quarter, San Diego, California.
FIGURES	All drawings by Donna Salmon.
PHOTOGRAPHS	All photographs by the authors unless otherwise noted.

Note: The U. S. Geological Survey is referred to as USGS. The National Oceanic and Atmospheric Adminstration/Environmental Data and Information Service is referred to as NOAA/EDIS.

Index